LEARNING GERMAN FOR BEGINNERS

1222 Phrases to Learn German and Grow your Vocabulary in the Easiest and Most Effective Way!

(Complete German Phrasebook)

John Alfort

Copyright © 2020 by John Alfort

All rights reserved.

No part of this book may be reproduced, stored in a retrieval system, or transmitted in any form or by any means, electronic, mechanical, photocopying, recording, scanning, or otherwise, without the prior written permission of the publisher.

This book is dedicated to the people who mean more to me than anything in the world…my students.

TABLE OF CONTENTS

THE STORY OF JOHN

SOME TIPS TO READ WELL THE BOOK

USEFUL RULES FOR THE PRONUNCIATION

Chapter 1: BEZIEHUNGEN – RELATIONSHIPS

Chapter 2: ZEIT – TIME

Chapter 3: TIERE – ANIMALS

Chapter 4: ZAHLEN UND MAßE – NUMBERS AND MEASUREMENTS

Chapter 5: TAG AND ROUTINE – DAY AND ROUTINE

Chapter 6: ADJEKTIVE – ADJECTIVES

Chapter 7: WAS GIBT ES IN DER STADT? – WHAT IN THERE IN THE CITY?

Chapter 8: GELD – MONEY

Chapter 9: FARBEN – COLOURS

Chapter 10: LEBENSMITTEL – FOOD AND RESTORATION

Chapter 11: ZUHAUSE – HOUSE

Chapter 12: ÜBER DAS EINKAUFEN – ABOUT SHOPPING

Chapter 13: SCHÖNHEIT – BEAUTY

Chapter 14: KONVERSATION – CONVERSATION

Chapter 15: GEFÜHLE UND CHARAKTER – FEELINGS AND CHARACTER

Chapter 16: REISEN – TRAVEL

Chapter 17: GESCHÄFTLICH – BUSINESS

THE END OF THE BOOK

THE STORY OF JOHN ALFORT

Hi!

All I need is two minutes to introduce myself to you before we begin.

My name is John Alfort, 45 years old and born in Oxford, England to a German mother and English father.

I have always had a great passion for travel, different cultures and languages from way back as a child.

I have always considered knowing a second language to be of great advantage to a person.

To quote Federico Fellini: "A different language is a different vision of life".

I strongly agree with this quote.

I began to travel a lot from the age of 16, and one of these trips in particular changed my life forever.

At 19 I decided to spend 3 months of my life in Rome to learn Italian and gain new experiences.

Throughout those months I worked hard, studied several books and took very expensive training courses. Even so, at the end of my stay in Italy I still had great difficulties communicating with my new friends.

The problem was that I had spent most of my time trying to memorize complex grammatical rules (gerund, past tense...), without focusing on the most important aspect of the language: VOCABULARY.

In fact, to quote David Wilkins: "Communicating without grammar is difficult but communicating without words is impossible".

And even now I can confirm that, VOCABULARY IS FUNDAMENTAL, GRAMMAR COMES IN SECOND.

In that moment, at the young age of 19, disappointed and frustrated by my first failure, I decided that I would do everything I could to learn Italian, but above all, I decided what I wanted to do for the rest of my life: to become one of the greatest foreign language expert.

Today, 26 years later, I can say that I succeeded. My team and I have succeeded in creating a new and innovative method of learning languages in an easy and intuitive way, completely revolutionizing the traditional learning process.

At the onset of my career in language teaching I was on my own. I started by giving private tutorials in the city center in an old garage that my parents no longer used.

The first year I had 4 students. Only 4 students.

Nonetheless, I did not give up, I continued to teach and the results were soon evident.

It's been over 20 years and now I have a team of professionals, expert translators and teachers at my side.

We have together written many books, held seminars and private lessons in various cities and I can say with pride that over the years we have been able to help tens of thousands of people to learn a new language.

I hope you enjoy this book ☺.

SOME USEFUL TIPS FOR STUDYING THIS BOOK

Before you begin studying, first grab a pen or pencil so that you can write and make notes in this book.

Studies have shown that using a pen or pencil when reading makes the reader more attentive and stimulates the memory.

Emphasize, circle, highlight words, fold the corners of pages and take notes at the margins of the book so you can pick up the book in the future and reread the parts you thought were most important.

Personally, I've always had big problems doing this, because as a proper obsessive-compulsive perfectionist I've always hated ruining the books I read.

Later I realized that I needed to immerse myself into books, as the purpose of a book like this is not to remain untouched, but rather to maximize the value we get out of it.

I now write in all the books I read (*except novels*) so I can revisit and reread them at any time, bringing myself up to speed in all the key areas, without having to reread the whole book again.

So, go get a pen and continue reading (...and underline)!

Other practical tips I feel like sharing with you are:

- **IT'S NOT A COMPETITION**

Your goal should not be to finish the book as quickly as possible.

I have had some students write me emails and private messages over the years complimenting me with the same phrase: "great book, I finished it in 6 hours", "I finished it in 2 days".

I feel very pleased that my books are appreciated, but trying to finish a book in the shortest possible time is a mistake.

Take your time to read this book. Read it 2-3 times and absorb every single word in it.

- **READ ALOUD**

I highly recommend reading out loud if you have the opportunity.

The two great researchers Colin MacLeod and Noah Farrin have dedicated themselves to studying the effects of reading aloud and its relationship to learning.

The research involved 100 students from the University of Waterloo, Canada, who were given 80 words to read aloud. Most of them noted down the words they couldn't remember for safety.

The next test involved the analysis of 2 different methods of remembering words: reading them silently or reading them out loud.

The results were astonishing, with the researchers coming up with the so-called "production effect". Two weeks after the test, the same participants were given a series of words to indicate whether they were part of those read or memorized during the test. Those who had read aloud gave considerably more accurate answers.

Having said that, I wish you success in your study!

USEFUL RULES FOR THE PRONUNCIATION

The German alphabet is very similar to the English one, but there are some key differences in pronunciation. Here's a guide to each letter's pronunciation.

- A – Pronounced "Ah"
- B – "Bay"
- C – "Tsay"
- D – "Day"
- E – "Ay"
- F – "Eff"
- G – "Gay"
- H – "Haa"
- I – "Eeh"
- J – "Yot"
- K – "Kah"
- L – "Ell"
- M – "Em"
- N – "En"
- O – "Oh"
- P – "Pay"
- Q – "Koo"
- R – "Er" (approximate to the uvular German pronunciation)
- S – "Es"
- T – "Tay"
- U – "Ooh"
- V – "Fow"
- W – "Vay"
- X – "Ix"
- Y – "Uep-si-lohn"

- Z – "Tset"
- Ü – Pronounce the German I with your lips rounded like a U
- Ö – Similar to the "I" in "Girl."

Ä – Sounds like an "Eh"

ß – Double "s" sound. Called an *Esszet*.

Even though the German alphabet is similar to the English alphabet, it's important that you recognize the letters that are different and learn the differences in pronunciation in order to make your German understandable and enjoyable to listen to.

Likewise, there are a few letters that are completely foreign to native English speakers. They are really are not difficult to learn and master, but it does take practice.

HOW TO PRONOUNCE LONG GERMAN WORDS

German is famous for its long words, and most people assume that the length of the word determines its pronunciation difficulty.

This, however, is not always the case.

German is an agglutinating language, which means that words build off of each other. This actually gives you an advantage when learning to pronounce words because you can break each word down into smaller words to learn how to pronounce the larger one.

Sound difficult? It's not. I promise. Let's look at a few examples to get a grasp of this concept:

1. *Freundschaftsbeziehungen* – This word, made famous by Mark Twain, is actually composed of separate words, *Freundschaft* (friendship) + *Beziehungen* (relationships). By knowing each of these smaller words and breaking the large word into its constituent parts, the pronunciation becomes much easier. Just pronounce each part like it's usually pronounced and you'll be pronouncing the whole word correctly.
2. *Geschwindigkeitsbeschränkungen* – This intimidating word is actually very common and important, but it's also composed of several smaller words, making it much scarier. It just means "speed limit," but its 30 letters make it much more frightening than it ought to be. It's actually composed of two words that are each composed of smaller particles. These two words are *Geschwindigkeit* (speed) + *Beschränkungen* (restrictions).

As you can see, the compound words in German actually create a system that *helps* the learner rather than *hinders* them, but it helps to know the individual words so you can pronounce the longer ones with ease.

HOW TO PRONOUNCE GERMAN LETTER COMBINATIONS

One of the most difficult parts of mastering any language's pronunciation is learning its letter combinations. Letter combinations are the sounds that certain letters make when they're next to one or more other specific letters.

German has quite a few distinct letter combinations, but they are consistent and none of them are too difficult to pronounce:

1. **Tsch** – This is a common combination and can be seen in the word Deutsch. It's pronounced exactly like the English "ch" like in "couch."
2. **Sch** – Without the "t," this combination is simply pronounced like the English "sh" like in "shoe."
3. **Ch** – This is by far the hardest for English speakers, and it's pronounced almost like a cat hissing but not nearly as angry.
4. **Sp** – This is pronounced like an English "sh" plus "p." It is very simple.
5. **St** – Similar to "sp," this is like the English "sh" plus "t." This combination and the combination of "sp" only apply when they are at the beginning of the syllable. There are other scenarios when these words are pronounced differently. Otherwise, they are pronounced as follows.
6. **St** – For the middle or end of a syllable, this is pronounced as the "st" in "straight."
7. **Eu** – This diphthong is pronounced exactly like "Oi" in English.
8. **Ei** – This diphthong is pronounced like the English word "eye."
9. **Ie** – Another diphthong, but pronounced like the English long "e."
10. **Pf** – This interesting combination is produced by pronouncing a "p" and "f" sound as close together as possible.

HOW TO PRONOUNCE GERMAN CITY NAMES

German city names are important for every German student because they are likely to come up in most learning texts as well as conversations with native speakers from Germany.

Learning to pronounce German city names well is also a bonus for travel within Germany and will help the learner avoid sounding like a tourist or beginner.

1. Berlin
2. München
3. Köln
4. Frankfurt

These are the largest cities in Germany and will likely be the subject of most discussions about Germany, but they also demonstrate the methods for pronouncing German cities.

Vowels are pure and clear in German, which distinguishes German pronunciation from English. Pure vowels are the trick to correctly pronouncing German city names.

BEZIEHUNGEN

-

RELATIONSHIPS

1. Familie = Family

Meine Familie ist eng verbunden.
My family is tight.

2. Onkel = Uncle

Mein Onkel ist nett.
My uncle is nice.

3. Tante = Aunt

Meine Tante ist eine alte Dame
My aunt is an old lady.

4. Cousin = Cousin

Der Name meines Cousins ist Peter.
My cousin's name is Peter.

5. Mutter = Mother

Meine Mutter ist tot.
My mother is dead.

6. Vater = Father

Mein Vater lebt hier
My father lives here.

7. Mama = Mum

Meine Mama liebt das Meer.
My mum loves the sea.

8. Papa = Dad

Mein Papa liebt Hunde
My dad loves dogs.

9. Großvater = Grandfather

Mein Großvater liebt Katzen.
My grandfather loves cats.

10. Großmutter = Grandmother

Meine Großmutter liebt das Kochen.
My grandmother loves cooking.

11. Großeltern = Grandparents

Meine Großeltern warden morgen ankommen.
My grandparents will arrive tomorrow.

12. Schwägerin = Sister-in-law

Meine Schwägerin ist Amerikanerin.
My sister-in-law is American.

13. Schwager = Brother-in-law

Mein Schwager hat rotes Haar.
My brother-in-law has red hair.

14. Schwiegertochter = Daughter-in-law

Meine Schwiegertochter kocht sehr gut.
My daughter-in-law cooks very well.

15. Schwiegersohn = Son-in-law

Sein Schwiegersohn ist eine sehr clevere Person.
His son-in-law is a very smart person.

16. Schwiegervater = Father-in-law

Gestern habe ich meinen Schwiegervater besucht. Er hat mir Nudeln gekocht.
Yesterday I went to visit my father-in-law. He cooked me pasta.

17. Schwiegermutter = Mother-in-law

Meine Schwiegermutter liebt Shoppen.
My mother-in-law loves shopping.

18. Sohn = Son

Marios Sohn studiert in England, und er spricht sehr gut Englisch.
Mario's son studies in England and he speaks English very well.

19. Tochter = Daughter

Meine Tochter ist eine sehr bekannte Schriftstellerin.
My daughter is a very well-known writer.

20. Einzelkind = Only child

Mario ist ein Einzelkind, weil seine Eltern zu alt waren, um noch weitere Kinder zu bekommen.
Mario is an only child because his parents were too old to have other children.

21. Nichte = Niece

Meine Nichte liebt das Schwimmen.
My niece loves swimming.

22. Neffe = Nephew

Der Name meines Neffen ist Carlo.
My nephew's name is Carlo.

23. Enkeltochter oder Enkelsohn = Granddaughter or Grandson

Ich liebe meinen Enkelsohn und meine Enkeltochter. Ich spiele oft mit ihnen.
I love my grandson and my granddaughter; I often play with them.

24. Schwester = Sister

Meine Schwester ist clever.
My sister is smart.

25. Bruder = Brother

Mein Bruder ist eifersüchtig.
My brother is jealous.

26. Verwandte = Relatives

Meine Verwandten werden morgen ankommen.
My relatives will arrive tomorrow.

27. Freundschaft = Friendship

Freundschaft ist eine großartige Sache.
Friendship is a magnificent thing.

28. Freund = Friend

Marco ist mein Freund.
Marco is my friend.

29. Freundin = Friend

Laura ist meine Freundin
Laura is my friend.

30. Feind = Enemy

In Breaking Bad ist Tuco Walters Feind.
In Breaking Bad, Tuco is Walter's enemy.

31. Rivale = Rival

Mattia ist der romantische Rivale von Marco.
Mattia is Marco's romantic rival.

32. Bester Freund = Best friend

Luca ist mein bester Freund
Luca is my best friend.

33. Freundin = Girlfriend

Roberta ist Matteos Freundin.
Matteo's girlfriend is Roberta.

34. Freund = Boyfriend

Matteo ist Robertas Freund.
Roberta's boyfriend is Matteo.

35. Ehemann = Husband

Gestern wurde Mirko zum Ehemann von Michela.
Yesterday Mirko became Michela's husband.

36. Ehefrau = Wife

Gestern wurde Michela zur Ehefrau von Mirko.
Yesterday Michela became Mirko's wife.

37. Bindung = Bond

Freundschaft ist eine sehr starke Bindung.
Friendship is a very strong bond.

38. Junge = Boy

Er ist 14 Jahre alt, er ist noch ein Junge.
He is 14 years old, he's just a boy.

39. Mädchen = Girl

Sie ist 12 Jahre alt; sie ist ein Mädchen.
She is 12 years old; she is a girl.

40. Ehe = Marriage

Unsere Ehe ist eine glückliche Ehe.
Our marriage is a happy one.

41. Paar = Couple

Wir sind ein echtes Paar.
We are a real couple.

42. Scheidung = Divorce

Eine Scheidung ist für Kinder traumatisch.
Divorce is traumatic for children.

43. Umarmen = To hug

Ich umarme immer meine Tochter.
I always hug my daughter.

44. Lieben = To love

Ich liebe Erdbeeren!
I love strawberries!

45. Bewundern = To admire

Mara bewundert deine Arbeit.
Mara admires your work.

46. Küssen = To kiss

Die Mutter küsst das Baby.
The mom kisses the baby.

47. Heiraten = To marry

John heiratete Maria.
John married Maria.

TIME
-
ZEIT

48. Montag = Monday

Heute ist Montag
Today is Monday.

49. Dienstag = Tuesday

Morgen wird Dienstag sein.
Tomorrow will be Tuesday.

50. Mittwoch = Wednesday

Ich fahre am Mittwoch nach Holland.
I am going to Holland on Wednesday.

51. Donnerstag = Thursday

Meine Mutter ist am Donnerstag gestorben.
My mom died on Thursday.

52. Freitag = Friday

Am Freitag wird es sonnig sein.
On Friday it will be sunny.

53. Samstag = Saturday

Am Samstag werde ich zur Schule gehen.
On Saturday I will go to school.

54. Sonntag = Sunday

Sonntag ist mein Ruhetag.
Sunday is my day of rest.

55. Sekunde = Second

Dieses Auto kann von 0 auf 100 km/h in weniger als 7 Sekunden beschleunigen.
This car can go from 0 to 100 km/h in less than 7 seconds.

56. Minute = Minute

Wir hatten noch sieben Minuten bis zum Beginn der Prüfung.
We had seven minutes to go before the start of the exam.

57. Stunde = Hour

Es dauert zweieinhalb Stunden, um dort anzukommen.
It takes two and a half hours to arrive there.

58. Voraus = Advance

Der Zug kam zehn Minuten im Voraus an.
The train arrived ten minutes in advance.

59. Zeitmesser = Chronometer

Ich benutze den Zeitmesser, um meine Rede zu üben.
I use the chronometer to practice my speech.

60. Zeit = Time

Die Abfahrtszeit muss noch festgelegt werden.
The departure time is still to be determined.

61. Mitternacht = Midnight

Warum schläfst du nicht?! Es ist Mitternacht.

Why aren't you sleeping?! It's midnight.

62. Zwölf Uhr = Twelve o'clock

Es ist zwölf Uhr, und ich würde jetzt gerne eine Pizza essen.
It's twelve o'clock and I would like to eat a pizza right now.

63. Viertel nach acht Uhr abends = Quarter past eight p.m.

Gestern habe ich um Viertel nach acht abends zu Abend gegessen.
Yesterday I had dinner at a quarter past eight p.m.

64. Halb vier Uhr nachmittags = Half past three p.m.

Ich ging um halb vier Uhr nachmittags zu Marco.
I went to Marco's at half past three p.m.

65. Fünf Uhr = Five o'clock

Gestern bin ich um fünf Uhr aufgewacht.
Yesterday I woke up at five o'clock.

66. Sommerzeit = Daylight saving time

In den meisten Ländern gilt im Sommer die Sommerzeit, allerdings mit unterschiedlichen Anfangszeiten.
Most countries have daylight saving time during summer, although with different beginning dates.

67. Sonnenzeit = Solar time

Ich habe nie verstanden, wie die Sonnenzeit funktioniert.
I have never understood how solar time works.

68. Countdown = Countdown

Die Menge hielt den Atem an, als der Countdown für den Start begann.
The crowd held their breath as the countdown to launch began.

69. Ortszeit = Local time

Das Flugzeug sollte um 4 Uhr morgens Ortszeit landen.
The plane should land at 4 a.m. local time.

70. Zeitzone = Time zone

Meine Freundin lebt in einer anderen Zeitzone, daher kann ich sie nur morgens anrufen.
My friend lives in a different time zone, so I can only call her in the morning.

71. Januar = January

Januar ist immer der kälteste Monat.
January is always the coldest month.

72. Februar = February

Februar ist mein Geburtstagsmonat!
February is my birthday month!

73. März = March

Im März beginnt der Frühling und die Blumen blühen.
In March, spring begins and flowers bloom.

74. April = April

Im April ist das Wetter immer wechselhaft.
In April, the weather is always unstable.

75. Mai = May

Der Mai ist ein wichtiger Monat für die katholische Religion.
May is an important month for the Catholic religion.

76. Juni = June

Im Juni ist die Schule vorbei.
In June schools are over.

77. Juli = July

Im Juli bringen alle Großmütter ihre Kinder an das Meer.
In July all grandmas take children to the seaside.

78. August = August

Im August sind Unternehmen geschlossen.
In August companies are closed.

79. September = September

Im September geht es wieder in die Schulen: Es ist Zeit zum Lernen.

In September schools are back: it's time to study.

80. Oktober = October

Im Oktober kommt endlich der Herbst.
In October autumn finally arrives.

81. November = November

Im November ist der Himmel immer grau.
In November the sky is always grey.

82. Dezember = December

Im Dezember ist es Zeit für Weihnachten und Silvester.
In December it's time for Christmas and New Year's Eve.

83. Frühling = Spring

Der Frühling ist voll von Düften und Farben.
Spring is full of scents and colours.

84. Sommer = Summer

Der Sommer ist die Zeit, in der die schönsten Früchte reifen.
Summer is when the smoothest fruits ripen.

85. Herbst = Autumn

Im Herbst sind alle Hügel in tausend Farbtönen gefärbt und sehen wie Bilder aus.
In autumn all hills are coloured by thousand shades and they look like pictures.

86. Winter = Winter

Im Winter spiele ich mit Schnee.
In winter I play with snow.

87. Frohes neues Jahr! = Happy New Year!

Nach dem Trinkspruch: Frohes neues Jahr!
After the toast, Happy New Year!

88. Frohe Weihnachten = Merry Christmas!

Ich danke Ihnen allen für Ihr Kommen und wünsche Ihnen frohe Weihnachten!
I thank you all for coming and Merry Christmas!

89. Frohe Ostern = Happy Easter!

Dies ist eine Gelegenheit, Ihnen frohe Ostern zu wünschen!
This is an occasion to wish you a Happy Easter!

90. Frohe Feiertage! = Happy Holidays!

Frohe Feiertage euch allen!
Happy Holidays to you all!

91. Silvester = New Year's Eve

Wo werden wir Silvester feiern?
Where will we celebrate New Year's Eve?

92. Karneval = Carnival

Karneval ist das Fest, bei dem alle jemand anders sein können.

Carnival is the feast where all can be someone else.

93. Weihnachten = Christmas

Weihnachten ist am 25. Dezember.
Christmas Day is on December 25th.

94. Tag der Befreiung = Liberation day

Der 25. April ist der Tag der Befreiung.
Liberation Day is on April 25th.

95. Osterhase = Easter bunny

Eines der Ostersymbole ist der Osterhase.
One of Easter symbols is the Easter bunny.

96. Palmsonntag = Palm Sunday

Am Palmsonntag werden die Olivenbäume gesegnet.
During Palm Sunday olive trees are blessed.

97. Dreikönigstag = Epiphany

Der Dreikönigstag findet am 6. Januar statt.
Epiphany occurs on January 6th.

98. Ferragosto = Mid-August Holiday

An Ferragosto essen wir alle zusammen.
On Mid-August Holiday we all eat together.

99. Vatertag = Father's Day

Meine Tochter hat den Vatertag sehr gern.

Father's Day is well-liked by my daughter.

100. Tag der Frauen = Women's Day

Der Tag der Frauen ist ein glücklicher Tag.
Woman's Day is a happy day.

101. Muttertag = Mother's Day

Der Muttertag ist ein schönes Fest.
Mother's Day is a sweet feast.

102. Halloween = Halloween

Gehst du an Halloween für Süßes oder Saures aus?
Will you go out for trick or treat on Halloween?

103. Feierlichkeit = Festivity

Jede Feierlichkeit ist eine Gelegenheit zum Feiern.
Every festivity is a chance to celebrate.

104. Ostern = Easter

Ostern bringt den späten Frühling mit sich.
Easter brings the late spring along.

105. Valentinstag = Valentine's Day

Der Valentinstag ist das Fest der Verliebten.
Valentine's Day is the lovers feast.

106. Schenken = To give

Was wirst du deinen Eltern zu Weihnachten schenken?

What will you give to your parents for Christmas?

107. Feiern = To celebrate

Meine Familie und ich feiern den Silvesterabend gemeinsam.
My family and I celebrate New Year's Eve all together.

ANIMALS
-
TIERE

108. Säugetiere = Mammals

Der Delphin ist ein Säugetier.
The dolphin is a mammal.

109. Reptilien = Reptile

In der Familie der Reptilien sind einige giftig.
In the family of reptiles some are poisonous.

110. Fische = Fishes

Im Aquarium gibt es eine Menge Fische.
In the aquarium there are a lot of fishes.

111. Schalentiere = Shellfish

An den Ufern findet man viele Schalentiere.
On the shores you can find many shellfish.

112. Muscheln = Clams

Quallen gehören zur Familie der Muscheln.
Jellyfish are part of the clams' family.

113. Käfer = Bugs

Ich habe viele Käferbisse.
I have many bugs bites.

114. Nutztiere = Farm animals

Mein Onkel hat viele Nutztiere.
My uncle has many farm animals.

115. Wilde Tiere = Wild animals

Im Dschungel leben wilde Tiere.
Wild animals live in the jungle.

116. Haustiere = Pets

In der Nähe meines Hauses gibt es ein Geschäft für Haustiere.
Near my home there is a pet shop.

117. Hund = Dog

Mario hat einen lebhaften Hund.
Mario has a lively dog.

118. Pferd = Horse

Das Pferd ist ein intelligentes Tier.
The horse is an intelligent animal.

119. Hase = Rabbit

Der Hase ist ein neugieriges Tier.
The rabbit is a curious animal.

120. Hamster = Hamster

Der Hamster hat scharfe Zähne.
The hamster has sharp teeth.

121. Henne = Hen

Die Henne legt Eier.
The hen makes eggs.

122. Hahn = Rooster

Jeden Morgen höre ich den Hahn singen.
Every morning I hear the rooster singing.

123. Katze = Cat

Die Katze ist ein Haustier.
The cat is a pet.

124. Schwein = Pig

Luigi hat sechs Schweine auf seinem Hof.
Luigi has six pigs in his farm.

125. Kuh = Cow

Auf den Bergweiden gibt es Kühe.
In the mountain pastures there are cows.

126. Truthahn = Turkey

Marco hat sieben Truthähne auf seinem Hof.
Marco has seven turkeys in his farm.

127. Maus = Mouse

Die Maus frisst Käse.
The mouse eats cheese.

128. Esel = Donkey

Mein Onkel hat einen Esel auf seinem Hof.
My uncle has a donkey in his farm.

129. Ochse = Ox

Das Mädchen ist stark wie ein Ochse.
That girl is as strong as an ox.

130. Maulesel = Mule

Der Maulesel ist sehr aggressiv.
That mule is very aggressive.

131. Ziege = Goat

Mein Bruder will eine Ziege kaufen!
My brother wants to buy a goat!

132. Schaf = Sheep

Dieses Schaf ist weiß und das andere ist schwarz.
That sheep is white and that other one is black.

133. Hirsch = Deer

Der Hirsch hat starke Beine.
The deer has strong legs.

134. Elefant = Elephant

Der Elefant trinkt mit seinem Rüssel.
The elephant drinks with its trunk.

135. Löwe = Lion

Der Löwe brüllt.
The lion roars.

136. Bär = Bear

Der Bär ist ein einsames Tier.
The bear is a lone animal.

137. Frosch = Frog

Der Frosch ist eine Amphibienart.
The frog is an amphibian.

138. Affe = Monkey

In einigen Kulturen ist der Affe ein Haustier.
In some cultures, the monkey is a pet.

139. Eichhörnchen = Squirrel

In den Stadtparks gibt es einige Eichhörnchen.
In the city gardens there are some squirrels.

140. Schlange = Snake

Ich habe in der Nähe meines Hauses eine Schlange gesehen.
I saw a snake near home.

141. Fuchs = Fox

Ich habe einen Fuchs in der Nähe unseres Hauses gesehen.
I saw a fox near our house.

142. Wal = Whale

Der Wal ist ein Säugetier.
The whale is a mammal.

143. Delfin = Dolphin

Der Delphin hat einen langen und beweglichen Körper.
The dolphin has a long and agile body.

144. Krabbe = Crab

Es gibt verschiedene Arten von Krabben.
There are different types of crabs.

145. Fisch = Fish

Goldfische werden von einigen Menschen als Haustiere angesehen.
The goldfish are considered pets by some people.

146. Hai = Shark

Vielleicht findest du einige Haie jenseits des Riffs.
You might find some sharks beyond the reef.

147. Schildkröte = Turtle

Jedes Jahr setzen wir uns für die Rettung von Schildkröten ein.
Every year we are committed to saving some turtles.

148. Tunfisch = Tuna

Der Thunfischfang ist eine traditionelle Beschäftigung in Sizilien.
Tuna fishing is a traditional activity in Sicily.

149. Lachs = Salmon

Hast du den Lachs gesehen? Der war riesig!
Have you seen that salmon? It's huge!

150. Wolfsbarsch = Bass

Dieser Wolfsbarsch ist sehr groß.
That bass is very big.

151. Dorade = Sea bream

Ich habe gestern eine Dorade gekauft.
I bought a sea bream yesterday.

152. Forelle = Trout

Magst du Forelle?
Do you like trout?

153. Seezunge = Sole

Mein Freund Freddy mag keine Seezungen.
My friend Freddy doesn't like sole.

154. Oktopus = Octopus

Kannst du den Oktopus da drüben sehen?
Can you see that octopus over there?

155. Hummer = Lobster

Hummer ist sehr teuer.
Lobster is very expensive.

156. Garnele = Shrimp

Garnelen gehen rückwärts.

Shrimps walk backwards.

157. Schwertfisch = Swordfish

Schwertfisch ist sehr lecker.
Swordfish is very tasty.

158. Adler = Eagle

Der Adler hat große Flügel.
The eagle has large wings.

159. Taube = Dove

Die Taube ist ein Symbol des Friedens.
The dove is a symbol of peace.

160. Möwe = Seagull

Es gibt eine Menge Möwen in der Nähe des Meeres.
There are a lot of seagulls near the sea.

161. Papagei = Parrot

Francesca hat einen sehr bunten Papagei.
Francesca has a very colorful parrot.

162. Taube = Pigeon

Die Plätze sind voller Tauben.
Squares are full of pigeons.

163. Vogel = Bird

Heute habe ich einen Schwarm von Vögeln gesehen.

Today I have seen a flock of birds.

164. Biene = Bee

Die Biene produziert Honig.
The bee produces honey.

165. Ameise = Ant

Die Ameise ist ein fleißiges Tier.
The ant is a hardworking animal.

166. Schmetterling = Butterfly

Es gibt viele Arten von Schmetterlingen.
There are many species of butterflies.

167. Spinne = Spider

Manche Spinnen sind giftig.
Some spiders are poisonous.

168. Bellen = To bark

Dein Hund hört nicht auf zu bellen! Ist er auf jemanden wütend?
Your dog won't stop barking! Is it angry with someone?

169. Miauen = To meow

Ich liebe meine Katze. Jedes Mal, wenn ich mein Haus verlasse, fängt sie an zu miauen.
I love my cat. Every time I leave my house it starts meowing.

170. Brüllen = To bellow

Ich bin auf einem Bauernhof aufgewachsen, und ich erinnere mich, dass ich morgens die Kühe brüllen hörte.
I grew up in a farm and I remember that in the morning I could hear the cows bellowing.

171. Wiehern = To whinny

Das Pferd wiehert, wenn es hungrig ist.
That horse whinnies when it's hungry.

172. Quieken = To squeak

Welches Geräusch macht eine Maus? Die Maus quiekt!
What sound does a mouse make? The mouse squeaks!

173. Summen = To buzz

Ich hasse diese Mücken! Sie summen immer um mich herum.
I hate these mosquitos! They always buzz around me.

174. Züchter = Breeder

Mein Vater ist ein Schweinezüchter. Was ist dein Vater von Beruf?
My father is a pig breeder. What's your father's job?

175. Katzenlady = Cat lady

Meine Mutter sagt mir immer, dass ich eine Katzenlady werden werde.
My mother always tells me I will become a cat lady.

176. Tierarzt = Vet

Wir bringen den Hund zum Tierarzt.
We are taking the dog to the vet.

177. Fischer = Fisherman

Die Fischer fahren vor Sonnenaufgang hinaus.
Fishermen go out before the sunrise.

NUMBERS AND MEASUREMENTS
-
ZAHLEN UND MAßE

178. Gerade Zahl = Even number

Die Zahl sechzehn ist eine gerade Zahl.
The number sixteen is an even number.

179. Ungerade Zahl = Odd number

Die Zahl 13 ist eine ungerade Zahl.
The number 13 is an odd number.

180. Kardinalzahl = Cardinal number

Die Zahl 99 ist eine Kardinalzahl.
The number 99 is a cardinal number.

181. Ordinalzahl = Ordinal number

Die Zweite ist eine Ordinalzahl.
Second is an ordinal number.

182. natürliche Zahl = Finite number

Eine Zahl ohne Dezimalstellen ist eine natürliche Zahl.
A number without decimals is a finite number.

183. Primzahl = Prime number
Die Zahl drei ist eine Primzahl.
The number three is a prime number.

184. Relative Zahl = Relative number

Die Zahl -3 ist eine relative Zahl.
The number -3 is a relative number.

185. Reihe von Zahlen = Set of numbers

Heute bestand die Aufgabe darin, eine Reihe von Zahlen zu erstellen.
Today the task was to create a set of numbers.

186. Irrationale Zahl = Irrational number

Pi ist eine so genannte irrationale Zahl.
Pi is what's known as an irrational number.

187. Zufällige Zahl = Random number

Heute werden wir eine zufällige Zahl extrahieren.
Today we will be extracting a random number.

188. Hausnummer = House number

In dieser Straße gibt es keine Hausnummern.
In this street there aren't house numbers.

189. Telefonnummer = Phone number

Meine Telefonnummer ist nicht verfügbar.
My phone number is not available.

190. Kreditkartennummer = Credit cart number

Ich brauche Ihre Kreditkartennummer für die Zahlung.
I need your credit card number for payment.

191. Postleitzahl = Zip code

Meine Postleitzahl ist 20100.
My zip code is 20100.

192. Breitengrad = Latitude

Es sollte etwas über den Breitengrad sagen.
It should say something about latitude.

193. Längengrad = Longitude

Die erste Zahl ist ein Längengrad.
The first number is a longitude.

194. Ausweisnummer = I.D. number

Seine Ausweisnummer lautet 03.
His I.D. number is 03.

195. Nummer Eins = Number one

Die Säuberung des Badezimmers hat im Moment Priorität Nummer eins.
Cleaning the bathroom is my number one priority right now.

196. Nummer Zwei = Number two

Das ist die Nummer Zwei.
This is the number two.

197. Nummer Drei = Number three

Nummer Drei bitte kommen.
Number three please come.

198. Nummer Vier = Number four

Nummer Vier ist sehr stark.

Number four is very strong.

199. Nummer Fünf = Number five

Du bekommst das T-Shirt mit der Nummer Fünf.
You will have the number five t-shirt.

200. Nummer Sechs = Number six

Morgen wird es die Nummer Sechs sein.
Tomorrow there will be number six.

201. Nummer Sieben = Number seven

Nummer Sieben ist eine Glückszahl.
Number seven is a lucky one.

202. Nummer Acht = Number eight

Die Nummer Acht ist ein Objekt im Vintage-Stil.
The number eight is a vintage style object.

203. Nummer Neun = Number nine

Wir sind bei Nummer Neun angekommen.
We arrived at number nine.

204. Nummer Zehn = Number ten

Wenn du mir die Nummer Zehn gibst, werde ich glücklich sein.
If you give me the number ten, I'll be happy.

205. Elf = Eleven

Wie alt ist deine Schwester? Elf Jahre?

How old is your sister? Eleven?

206. Zwölf = Twelve

Wie viele Leute werden heute Abend auf der Party sein? Zwölf?
How many people are going to be at the party tonight? Twelwe?

207. Dreizehn = Thirteen

Mein Sohn ist dreizehn Jahre alt, aber er ist sehr klug.
My son is thirteen years old, but he is very smart.

208. Vierzehn = Fourteen

Dieses Jahr habe ich vierzehn Kilo abgenommen.
This year I've lost fourteen kilos.

209. Fünfzehn = Fifteen

Meine Mutter und mein Vater sind seit fünfzehn Jahren verheiratet.
My mother and my father have been married for fifteen years.

210. Sechzehn = Sixteen

Kannst du mir sechzehn Äpfel geben?
Could you give me sixteen apples?

211. Siebzehn = Seventeen

Dein Bruder wurde vor siebzehn Jahren geboren.
Your brother was born seventeen years ago.

212. Achtzehn = Eighteen

Ich bin jetzt achtzehn Jahre alt und kann allein in den Urlaub fahren.
I'm eighteen now and I can go on holiday by myself.

213. Neunzehn = Nineteen

Die Neunzehn ist meine Glückszahl.
Ninteen is my lucky number.

214. Zwanzig = Twenty

Piero hat zwanzig Klassenkameraden.
Piero has twenty classmates.

215. Einundzwanzig = Twenty-one

In den USA kann man keinen Alkohol kaufen, wenn man unter einundzwanzig Jahre alt ist.
In America, you can't buy alcohol if you aren't at least twenty-one years old.

216. Zweiundzwanzig = Twenty-two

Ich habe dieses Buch gekauft. Es kostet zweiundzwanzig Euro.
I bought this book. It costs twenty-two euros.

217. Dreiundzwanzig = Twenty-three

Maria ist dreiundzwanzig Jahre alt und lebt allein.
Maria is twenty-three years old and she lives alone.

218. Vierundzwanzig = Twenty-four

Marisa und ihr Freund sind vierundzwanzig Jahre alt.
Marisa and her boyfriend are twenty-four years old.

219. Fünfundzwanzig = Twenty-five

Gestern Abend haben wir fünfundzwanzig Weinflaschen verkauft.
Last night we sold twenty-five wine bottles.

220. Sechsundzwanzig = Twenty-six

Ich wurde am sechsundzwanzigsten Juni 1998 geboren.
I was born on the twenty-sixth of June 1998.

221. Siebenundzwanzig = Twenty-seven

Ich muss noch die nächsten siebenundzwanzig Jahre arbeiten.
I must work for the next twenty-seven years.

222. Achtundzwanzig = Twenty-eight

Meine Lieblingszahl ist achtundzwanzig, doch ich kann dir nicht sagen, warum!
My favourite number is twenty-eight, but I can't tell you why!

223. Neunundzwanzig = Twenty-nine

Wie alt ist dein Onkel? Meiner Meinung nach ist er neunundzwanzig Jahre alt.
How old is your uncle? In my opinion he is twenty-nine years old.

224. Dreißig = Thirty

Ich habe im Supermarkt dreißig Liter Bier gekauft.
I bought thirty litres of beer at the supermarket.

225. Einunddreißig = Thirty-one

Meine Mutter ist einunddreißig Jahre alt.
My mum is thirty-one years old.

226. Vierzig = Fourty

Ich brauche vierzig Tage Urlaub!
I need a fourty days holiday!

227. Fünfzig = Fifty

In dieser Schule gibt es fünfzig Schülerinnen und Schüler. Sie ist sehr klein!
There are fifty students in this school. It's very small!

228. Achtundfünfzig = Fifty-eight

Die Achtundfünfzig ist meine Glückszahl.
Fifty-eight is my lucky number.

229. Einhundert = One hundred

Kannst du mir bitte 100 Euro geben? Ich brauche sie für die Bücher.
Could you give me one hundred dollars please? I need them for the books.

230. Einhundertfünfzehn = One hundred fifteen

Mein Großvater starb im Alter von einhundertfünfzehn Jahren.
My granddad died at one hundred fifteen years.

231. Einhundertfünfundsiebzig = One hundred seventy-five

Im Zoo gibt es einhundertfünfundsiebzig Tiere.
At the zoo there are one hundred seventy-five animals.

232. Eintausend = One thousand

Ich habe schon eintausend Mal versucht, dieses Problem zu lösen, aber ich kann die Lösung nicht finden.
I have tried to solve this problem one thousand times, but I can't find the solution.

233. Eintausendvierhundert = One thousand four hundred

Ich war auf einer Party mit eintausendvierhundert Gästen.
I was at a party with one thousand four hundred guests.

234. Eintausend-neunhundertzweiundzwanzig = One thousand nine hundred twenty-two

In meiner Stadt gibt es eintausendneunhundertzweiundzwanzig Einwohner.
In my city there are one thousand nine hundred twenty-two inhabitants.

235. = Zehntausend

Reichen zehntausend Euro, um dieses Auto zu bezahlen?

Are ten thousand dollars enough to pay this car?

236. = Hunderttausend

Dieses Haus kostet hunderttausend Euro.
This house costs a hundred thousand dollars.

237. Drei Millionen = Three million

Der Lotteriegewinn beträgt diese Woche drei Millionen Euro.
The lottery prize is three million euros this week.

238. Sieben Milliarden = Seven billion

Auf der Erde gibt es sieben Milliarden Menschen.
There are seven billion people on Earth.

239. Erste = First

Ich habe den ersten Platz belegt.
I placed first.

240. Zweite = Second

Ich war in meinem zweiten Jahr der Oberstufe.
I was in my second year of high school.

241. Dritte = Third

Ich werde immer Dritter.
I always place third.

242. Vierte = Fourth

Gary wurde beim Schwimmwettbewerb Vierter.
Gary finished fourth at the swimming competition.

243. Fünfte = Fifth

Vettel qualifizierte sich als Fünfter.
Vettel qualified fifth.

244. Sechste = Sixth

Ich war der sechste meiner Klasse.
I was the sixth of my class.

245. Siebte = Seventh

Ich gehöre der siebten Generation meiner Familie an.
I am the seventh generation of my family.

246. Achte = Eighth

Dies ist der achte PC, den ich kaufe.
This is the eighth pc that I buy.

247. Neunte = Ninth

An der neunten Kreuzung biegen Sie rechts ab.
At the ninth intersection, turn right.

248. Zehnte = Tenth

John ist der zehnte Sohn von Theresa.
John is Theresa's tenth son.

249. Unendlich = Infinite

Unendlich ist eine große Zahl.
Infinite is a big number.

250. Bruch = Fraction

Der Bruch erzeugt eine Dezimalzahl.
The fraction generates a decimal number.

251. Prozentwert = Percentage

Der Prozentwert ist ein mathematisches Werkzeug, das zwei Größen in Beziehung setzt.
The percentage is a mathematical tool relating two quantities.

252. Division = Division

Die Division ist die umgekehrte Operation zur Multiplikation.
Division is the reverse operation to multiplication.

253. Multiplikation = Multiplication

Die Multiplikation ist die Gegenoperation zur Division.
Multiplication is the reverse operation to division.

254. Summe = Sum

Die Summe ist das Ergebnis der Additionsoperation.
The sum is the result of the addition operation.

255. Subtraktion = Subtraction

Heute muss ich in der Schule die Subtraktion lernen.
Today at school I must learn subtraction.

256. Mathematische Ableitungen = Mathematical derivations

Kannst du mathematische Ableitungen lösen?
Can you solve mathematical derivations?

257. Gleichung = Equation

Und das ist die Antwort auf die Gleichung.
And that's the answer to the equation. Number base

258. Integral = Integral

Integrale sind schwer zu lösen.
Integrals are hard to solve.

259. Größer = Greater

Eins ist größer als Null.
One is greater than zero.

260. Größter gemeinsamer Nenner = Highest common denominator

Der größte gemeinsame Nenner zwischen 4 und 3 ist 1.
The highest common denominator between 4 and 3 is 1.

261. Kleinstes gemeinsames Vielfaches = Least common multiple

Das kleinste gemeinsame Vielfache zwischen 3 und 2 ist 6.
The least common multiple between 3 and 2 is 6.

262. Kleiner = Minor

Drei ist kleiner als fünf.
Three is minor than five.

263. Quadratwurzel = Square root

Die Quadratwurzel aus 4 ist 2.
The square root of 4 is 2.

264. Zahlenbasis = Number base

Kannst du die Zahlenbasis ändern?
Can you change the number base?

265. Binärsystem = Binary system

Computer arbeiten mit einem Binärsystem.
Computers work with binary system.

266. Taschenrechner = Calculator

Ich kann den Taschenrechner während der Prüfung nicht benutzen.
I can't use the calculator during the exam.

267. Konstante = Constant

Pi ist eine mathematische Konstante.
Pi is a mathematical constant.

268. Passcode = Pass code

Der Passcode lautet 170419.
The pass code is 170419.

269. Numerische Reihe = Numerical series

Vervollständige die numerische Reihe.
Complete the numerical series.

270. Lineare Systeme = Linear system

Lineare Systeme sind leicht zu lösen.
Linear systems are easy to solve.

271. Satz = Theorem

Der Satz des Pythagoras wird dir helfen.
Pythagora's theorem will help you.

272. Meter = Metre

Wir müssen 600 Meter gehen.
We must walk for 600 metres.

273. Zentimeter = Centimetre

Du bist ein paar Zentimeter größer als ich.
You're a few centimetres taller than me.

274. Millimeter = Millimetre

Die Büroklammer ist einen Millimeter dick.
The paper clip is one millimetre thick.

275. Kilometer = Kilometre

Innerhalb eines Kilometers werden wir unser Ziel erreichen.

In a kilometre we will arrive at our destination.

276. Liter = Litre

Mein Aquarium enthält 200 Liter Wasser.
My aquarium contains 200 litres of water.

277. Dichte = Density

Eisen hat eine höhere Dichte als Holz.
Iron has a higher density than wood.

278. Größe = Height

Er ist ein Mann von durchschnittlicher Größe.
He is an average height man.

279. Tiefe = Depth

Hier hat das Wasser eine unbekannte Tiefe.
Here water has an unknow depth.

280. Distanz = Distance

Die Distanz beträgt 25 km.
It's a 25 km distance.

281. Länge = Length

Das Haus hatte eine Länge von 15 Metern.
The house had a 15 metres length.

282. Geschwindigkeit = Speed

Der Zug fährt mit einer Geschwindigkeit von 100 km/h.

The train travels at the speed of 100 km/h.

283. Leistung = Power

Der Motor eines Autos setzt eine Menge Leistung frei.
The engine of a car releases a lot of power.

284. Beschleunigung = Acceleration

Die Beschleunigung beschreibt, wie die Geschwindigkeit mit der Zeit zunimmt.
Acceleration describes how the speed increases in time.

285. Frequenz = Frequency

Meine Atemfrequenz ist sehr hoch.
My respiratory frequency is very high.

286. Masse = Mass

Deine Masse hat deutlich abgenommen, hast du eine Diät gemacht?
Your mass has decreased considerably, have you followed a diet?

287. Oberfläche = Surface

Diese Oberfläche des Gebäudes soll restauriert werden.
That building surface is to be restored.

288. Fläche = Area

Die Fläche eines Kreises hängt vom Radius ab.
The area of a circle depends on the radius.

289. Volumen = Volume

Das Volumen dieser Flasche ist sehr klein.
The volume of that bottle is very little.

290. Intensität = Intensity

Du besitzt eine große Trainingsintensität.
You have a great training intensity.

291. Gewicht = Weight

Das Gewicht meines Hundes ist durchschnittlich.
My dog's weight is average.

292. Kilogramm = Kilogram
Dieser Tisch wiegt 15 Kilogramm.
That table weighs 15 kilograms.

293. Dezigramm = Decigram

Mein Notizbuch wiegt 1 Dezigramm.
My notebook weighs 1 decigram.

294. Milligramm = Milligram

Milligramm wird zum Wiegen von kleinen Objekten verwendet.
Milligram is used to weigth small objects.

295. Gramm = Gram

Das Gramm ist die Grundeinheit der Masse.
The gram is the basic unit of mass.

296. Summieren = To sum

Mara summiert ihre Ausgaben.
Mara sums her expenses.

297. Multiplizieren = To multiply

Mit zwei multiplizieren.
Multiply by two.

298. Dividieren = To divide

Man kann eine Zahl nicht durch Null dividieren.
You can't divide a number by zero.

299. Abziehen = To deduct

Die Kassiererin zieht 2 Euro Rabatt ab.
The cashier deducts 2 euros discount.

300. Messen = To measure

Bill misst die Größe der Tür.
Bill measures the size of the door.

301. Zählen = To count

Johanna zählt das restliche Geld in der Geldbörse.
Johanna counts the remaining money in the wallet.

DAY AND ROUTINE
-
TAG UND ROUTINE

302. Morgendämmerung = Dawn

Heute Morgen wachte ich in der Morgendämmerung auf.
This morning I woke up at dawn.

303. Morgen = Morning

Ich wache jeden Morgen früh auf.
I wake up early every morning.

304. Nachmittag = Afternoon

Am Nachmittag wird mir oft langweilig.
I often get bored in the afternoon.

305. Abend = Evening

Am Abend sehe ich gerne auf dem Sofa fern.
In the evening I love watching TV on the sofa.

306. Sonnenuntergang = Sunset

I leave home at sunset.

307. Nacht = Night

Ich verlasse mein Zuhause zum Sonnenuntergang.
I go to bed late at night.

308. Aufwachen = To wake up

Jeden Morgen wache ich im Morgengrauen auf.
Every morning I wake up at dawn.

309. Frühstück = Breakfast

Ich esse Milch mit Müsli zum Frühstück.
I eat milk with cereals for breakfast.

310. Zähne putzen = To brush one's teeth

Ich putze mir jeden Morgen die Zähne.
I brush my teeth every morning.

311. Duschen = To get a shower

Ich dusche immer, wenn ich nach Hause komme.
I always get a shower when I come back home.

312. Sich anziehen = To dress

Ich ziehe mich immer hübsch an.
I always dress nicely.

313. Zur Arbeit gehen = To go to work

Ich gehe jeden Tag um 15:00 Uhr zur Arbeit.
I go to work every day at 3.00 PM.

314. Hausaufgaben machen = To do homework

Normalerweise mache ich meine Hausaufgaben, sobald ich von der Schule zurückkomme.
I usually do my homework as soon as I come back from school.

315. Mittagessen = Lunch

Ich esse immer ein Sandwich zum Mittagessen.
I always eat a sandwich for lunch.

316. Getränk = Drink

Wollen wir uns morgen auf ein Getränk treffen?
Shall we see tomorrow for a drink?

317. Abendbrot = Dinner

Ich koche das Abendessen für meine Großeltern.
I'm cooking dinner for my grandparents.

318. Im Web surfen = To surf the web

Ich surfe oft im Web.
I often surf the web.

319. Den Müll rausbringen = To take out the trash

Ich bringe immer den Müll raus.
I always take out the trash.

320. Entspannen = Relax

Sonntag ist mein Tag zum Entspannen.
Sunday is my relax day.

ADJECTIVES - ADJEKTIVE

321. Gebräunt = Tanned

Luca scheint gebräunt zu sein, war er am Meer?
Luca seems tanned, has he been to the sea?

322. Angenehm = Pleasant

Ich bin gerne in seiner Gesellschaft, weil er ein netter und angenehmer Mensch ist.
I like being in his company because he is a nice and pleasant person.

323. Liebevoll = Affectionate

Bonnie war schon immer ein liebevoller Mensch; sie liebt es, Menschen zu umarmen und ihre Hände zu halten.
Bonnie has always been an affectionate person; she loves hugging people and holding their hands.

324. Zuverlässig = Reliable

Sind diese Daten zuverlässig?
Is this data reliable?

325. Fröhlich = Cheerful

Fiona ist morgens normalerweise fröhlich.
Fiona is usually cheerful in the morning.

326. Hoch = Tall

Dieser Wolkenkratzer ist hoch, aber der neue Wolkenkratzer, den sie neben ihm bauen, wird noch höher sein.

That skyscraper is tall but the new one they're building beside will be even taller.

327. Ambitioniert = Ambitious

Sie war ambitioniert genug, um die Leitung des Unternehmens anzustreben.
She was ambitious enough to aim for the company's presidency.

328. Freundlich = Friendly

Er ist ein so freundlicher Mensch. Jeder mag ihn.
He's such a friendly person. Everyone likes him.

329. Unangenehm = Unpleasant

Der neue Freund meiner Schwester ist wirklich unangenehm.
My sister's new boyfriend is really unpleasant.

330. Arrogant = Arrogant

Der Vorgesetzte unserer Abteilung ist arrogant und unhöflich.
The supervisor of our department is arrogant and rude.

331. Vernünftig = Sensible

Er war ein vernünftiger Experte und man konnte ihm vertrauen.
He was a sensible professional and he could be trusted.

332. Athletisch = Athletic

Die Fußballspieler haben einen athletischen Körper.
The football players have an athletic body.

333. Autoritär = Authoritative

Sein autoritativer Ton brachte die ungehorsamen Schüler schnell wieder in die Reihe.
His authoritative tone quickly brought the unruly students back in line.

334. Gemein = Mean

Im Gegensatz zu seinem großzügigen Bruder ist er ein gemeiner Mann.
Unlike his generous brother, he is a mean man.

335. Abenteuerlustig = Adventurous

Ich bin nicht abenteuerlustig genug, um Fallschirmspringen auszuprobieren.
I'm not adventurous enough to try sky-diving.

336. Klein = Short

In meiner Familie sind wir alle sehr klein.
In my family we're all very short.

337. Wunderschön = Beautiful

Die Landschaft ist in Schottland wunderschön.
In Scotland, the landscape is very beautiful.

338. Wohlhabend = Wealthy

Ich hatte das Glück, in einer wohlhabenden Familie aufzuwachsen.
I was lucky enough to grow up in a wealthy family.

339. Brillant = Brilliant

Er war schon immer ein brillanter Schüler.
He's always been a brilliant student.

340. Schlecht = Bad

Ich fürchte, ich habe schlechte Nachrichten für dich.
I'm afraid I have some bad news for you.

341. Gut = Good

Er hat viel gelernt und in diesem Jahr gute Noten bekommen.
He studied hard and got good grades this year.

342. Ruhig = Calm

Er war trotz des Drucks, der auf ihm lastete, ruhig.
He was calm despite the pressure on him.

343. Schlecht = Bad

Der Fernsehempfang war schlecht.
The television reception was bad.

344. Pummelig = Chubby

Ellen war nicht übergewichtig, aber sie hielt sich für pummelig.

Ellen was not overweight, but she considered herself chubby.

345. Mutig = Brave

Die mutigen Soldaten stürzten sich auf das Schlachtfeld.
The brave soldiers rushed onto the battlefield.

346. Kreativ = Creative

Mein Kunstlehrer ist sehr kreativ und produziert wirklich originelle Kunstwerke.
My art teacher is very creative and produces really original works.

347. Entschlossen = Resolute

In seinen persönlichen Beziehungen ist er nie sehr entschlossen.
He's never very resolute in his personal relationships.

348. Bestimmt = Determined

Wenn ich etwas will, kann ich sehr bestimmt sein.
When I want something, I can be very determined.

349. Gutmütig = Sweet-tempered

Paola ist ein gutmütiges Mädchen.
Paola is a sweet-tempered girl.

350. Mittleren Alters = Middle-aged

Sie ist eine Frau mittleren Alters.
She is a middle-aged woman.

351. Diabolisch = Diabolical

Sein Gesicht lächelte freundlich, doch sein Lachen war diabolisch.
His face was smiling kindly, but his laugh was diabolical.

352. unparteiisch = Disinterested

Wir brauchen die Meinung einer unparteiischen Seite.
We need the opinion of a disinterested party.

353. Unehrlich = Dishonest

Wir müssen uns davor hüten, uns mit unehrlichen Freunden zu umgeben.
We must be careful not to surround ourselves with dishonest friends.

354. Böse = Naughty

Anthony ist ein böser Junge und er spielt immer böse Streiche.
Anthony is a naughty boy and he always plays bad tricks.

355. Hilfreich = Helpful

Sara ist immer ein nettes und hilfsbereites Mädchen.
Sara is always a nice and helpful girl.

356. Höflich = Polite

Höfliche Menschen streiten nicht in der Öffentlichkeit.
Polite people don't argue in public.

357. Egoistisch = Selfish

Sie wird das nicht für dich tun, weil sie sehr egoistisch ist.
She won't do that for you because she is very selfish.

358. Emotional = Emotional

Er ist ein emotionaler Mensch.
He is an emotional person.

359. Energiegeladen = Energetic

Kinder werden zu energiegeladen für ihre Großeltern.
Children are getting too energetic for their grandparents.

360. Enthusiastisch = Enthusiastic

Adam ist ein enthusiastischer Schüler, der im Klassenzimmer immer wieder interessante Fragen stellt.
Adam is an enthusiastic student who always asks interesting questions in the classroom.

361. Aufgeschlossen = Outgoing

Glenn ist aufgeschlossen. Sie liebt es, auf Partys zu gehen, und es macht ihr nichts aus, mit Fremden zu sprechen.
Glenn is outgoing; she loves going to parties and she doesn't mind talking to strangers.

362. Überschwänglich = Exuberant

Sallys überschwängliche Persönlichkeit zog viele Bewunderer an.
Sally's exuberant personality attracted many admirers.

363. Zuversichtlich = Confident

Ich bin nicht sehr zuversichtlich über das Ergebnis meines Gesprächs mit dem Beurteiler.
I'm not very confident about the outcome of my interview with the assessor.

364. Eifersüchtig = Jealous

Er war eifersüchtig auf seinen Bruder, der klüger und besser aussehend war als er.
He was jealous of his brother who was smarter and better looking than him.

365. Großzügig = Generous

Nate war großzügig zu seinen Freunden, aber er hat seine eigenen Bedürfnisse vernachlässigt.
Nate was generous to his friends, but he neglected his own needs.

366. Jung = Young

Er ist noch jung und muss noch eine Menge lernen.
He is still young and has a lot to learn.

367. Ignorant = Ignorant

Verschwenden wir nicht unsere Zeit damit, uns die Tiraden dieser ignoranten Gangster anzuhören.
Let's not waste our time listening to rants from those ignorant thugs.

368. Impulsiv = Impulsive

Mein Bruder ist impulsiv, er handelt immer ohne nachzudenken.
My brother is impulsive, he always acts without thinking.

369. Unsicher = Insecure

Seine unsichere Haltung war ein Zeichen von Schwäche
His insecure attitude was a sign of weakness.

370. Intelligent = Intelligent

Er war ein intelligentes Kind.
He was an intelligent child.

371. Introvertiert = Introverted

Mein Sohn ist ziemlich introvertiert; ich wünschte, er könnte etwas geselliger sein!
My son is quite introverted; I wish he could be more social!

372. Mühsam = Laborious

Es ist eine sehr mühsame Aufgabe.
It's a very laborious task.

373. Treu = Loyal

Er ist treu wie ein wahrer Freund
He's loyal like a true friend.

374. Redefreudig = Talkative

Der Lehrer trennte den redefreudigen Schüler von seinen Freunden.
The teacher separated the talkative pupil from his friends.

375. Launisch = Moody

Dan konnte ein bisschen launisch sein, deshalb war es wichtig, ihn bei Laune zu halten, wenn man etwas von ihm wollte.
Dan could be a bit moody, so it was important to keep him happy if you wanted anything from him.

376. Dünn = Thin

Der dünne Kerl da drüben verfolgt mich immer noch.
That thin guy over there is still following me.

377. Ungeschickt = Clumsy

Jake ist so ungeschickt: Er rennt immer in irgendwas hinein und lässt alles fallen, was er in die Hände bekommt.
Jake is so clumsy: he's always running into something and dropping whatever he brings in his hands.

378. Unhöflich = Rude

Es war unhöflich, so etwas zu sagen.
That was a rude thing to say.

379. Böse = Wicked

Das böse Kind quälte das Kätzchen.
The wicked child tormented the kitten.

380. Fest = Solid

Der Küchentisch ist aus festem Holz gefertigt.
The kitchen table is made of solid wood.

381. Erwachsen= Mature

Er war ein erwachsener Junge, obwohl er erst sechzehn Jahre alt war.
He was a mature boy though he was sixteen.

382. Ausgeglichen = Even-tempered

Mein Vater war ein ausgeglichener Mann, der nie seine Stimme erhob.
My father was an even-tempered man who never raised his voice.

383. Bescheiden = Modest

Kate war sehr bescheiden, und sie mochte nicht zu viel Aufmerksamkeit.
Kate was very modest, and she didn't like too much attention.

384. Nervös = Nervous

Ich bin vor einem Test immer nervös.
I am always nervous before a test.

385. Langweilig = Boring

Ich möchte diesen langweiligen Kurs verlassen.
I want to leave this boring class.

386. Übergewichtig = Obese

Sein übergewichtiger Körperbau erschwerte sogar das Gehen.
His obese physique made it difficult even to walk.

387. Ehrlich = Honest

Ein ehrlicher Mensch braucht sich nicht an das zu erinnern, was er gesagt hat.
An honest person has no need to remember what he said.

388. Schwerfällig = Dense

Ich hasse den Umgang mit schwerfälligen Menschen.
I hate dealing with dense people.

389. Geduldig = Patient

Um ein guter Angler zu sein, muss man geduldig sein.
To be a good angler you must be patient.

390. Verrückt = Mad

Er war verrückt und sie mussten ihn in eine psychiatrische Klinik schicken.
He was mad and they had to sent him to a psychiatric hospital.

391. Faul = Lazy

Er ist klug, aber faul.
He is smart, but lazy.

392. Praktisch = Practical

Belinda ist eine zu praktische Person, um eine gute Karriere für einen Mann wegzuwerfen.
Belinda is a too practical person to throw away a good career because of a man.

393. Dominant = Bossy

Karen wusste Lisas dominante Haltung nicht zu schätzen.
Karen didn't appreciate Lisa's bossy attitude.

394. Eingebildet = Conceited

Owen ist eingebildet und es ist schwierig, mit ihm zu reden.
Owen is conceited and difficult to talk to.

395. Vorsichtig = Cautious

Joe ist ein vorsichtiger Geschäftsmann; er geht nicht gerne Risiken ein.
Joe is a cautious businessman; he doesn't like to take risks.

396. Verantwortungsvoll = Responsible

Ja, Giovanni ist eine verantwortungsvolle Person.
Yes, Giovanni is a responsible person.

397. Nachdenklich = Reflective

Franco hat einen nachdenklichen Charakter.
Franco has a reflective character.

Zurückhaltend = Reserved

Lucia war schon immer ein sehr zurückhaltendes Mädchen.
Lucia has always been a very reserved girl.

398. Respektabel = Respectable

Roberto war ein ehrlicher und respektabler Mann.
Roberto was an honest and respectable man.

399. Engstirnig = Narrow-minded

Ich bin nicht so engstirnig, dass ich anderen meinen persönlichen Geschmack aufdränge.
I'm not so narrow-minded as to impose my personal taste on others.

400. Wählerisch = Fussy

Paul war sehr wählerisch, und er neigte dazu, Dinge nicht so schnell zu erledigen.
Paul was very fussy and he tended not to get things done very quickly.

401. Doof = Silly

Der Komiker war für seinen doofen Humor bekannt.
The comedian was known for his silly humour.

402. Ernst = Serious

Ich mache keine Witze. Ich meine es ernst.
I'm not joking. I'm serious.

403. Sicher = Sure

Ich bin mir nicht sicher, ob das eine gute Idee ist.
I'm not sure that it's a good idea.

404. Sympathisch = Likable

Giulio ist ein sympathischer Typ und wird von allen geliebt.
Giulio is a likable guy and he's loved by everyone.

405. Aufrichtig = Sincere

Das war definitiv kein aufrichtiges Lächeln.

406. Hochnäsig = Snobbish

Die Nachbarn meiden uns, weil sie hochnäsig sind.
The neighbours are avoiding us because they're snobbish.

407. Gesellig = Sociable

Die neuen Nachbarn scheinen sehr gesellig zu sein, meinst du nicht auch?
The new neighbours seem very sociable, don't you think?

408. Närrisch = Foolish

Ryan hat einen närrischen Fehler gemacht.
Ryan made a foolish mistake.

409. Dumm = Dumb

Sie war zu dumm, um sich eine Alternative auszudenken.
She was too dumb to think of an alternative.

410. Schrecklich = Terrible

Es war ein schreckliches Erlebnis.
It was a terrible experience.

411. Dickköpfig = Stubborn

Er war dickköpfig und weigerte sich, seinen Irrtum einzugestehen.
He was stubborn and refused to admit he was wrong.

412. Schüchtern = Shy

Das Mädchen war so schüchtern, dass sie sich versteckte, wenn jemand mit ihr sprach.
The girl was so shy that she hid when someone spoke to her.

413. Tolerant = Tolerant

Bislang war ich sehr tolerant.
So far, I've been tolerant.

414. Alt = Old

Der alte Zimmermann sollte in den Ruhestand gehen.
That old carpenter should retire.

415. Lebhaft = Lively

Er ist ein ziemlich lebhaftes Kind.
He is a rather lively child.

416. Schnell = Fast

Dieses Fahrrad ist wirklich schnell.
This bike is really fast.

WHAT IS THERE IN THE CITY?
-
WAS GIBT ES IN DER STADT?

417. Allee = Avenue

Die Allee von Buenos Aires ist voll von Geschäften.
Buenos Aires Avenue is full of shops.

418. Bushaltestelle = Bus stop

Ich warte auf dich an der Bushaltestelle.
I'm waiting for you at the bus stop.

419. Fußgängerüberweg = Pedestrian crossing

Am Fußgängerüberweg musst du anhalten.
You must stop at the pedestrian crossing.

420. Bürgersteig = Sidewalk

Bleib auf dem Bürgersteig, das ist sicherer.
Stay on the sidewalk, it's safer.

421. Bank = Bench

Ich bin früh dran, ich werde auf einer Bank sitzen und auf dich warten.
I'm early, I'll sit on a bench waiting for you.

422. Parken = Parking

Ich bin auf der Suche nach einem Parkplatz.
I'm looking for a parking spot.

423. Parkplatz = Car park

Die Zahl der Parkplätze wird immer kleiner.

Car parks are less and less.

424. Taxistand = Taxi rank

Wenn du zum Taxistand gehst, wirst du auch jemanden finden.
If you go to the taxi rank you can find someone.

425. Park = Park

Der Park schließt nachts.
The park closes at night.

426. Vororte = Suburbs

Die Vororte sind überbevölkert.
The suburbs are overpopulated.

427. Platz = Square

Es gibt viele Geschäfte auf dem Platz.
There are many shops in the square.

428. Hauptplatz = Main square

Wir sind auf dem Hauptplatz.
We are in the main square.

429. Öffentliches Schwimmbad = Public pool

Sie haben öffentliche Schwimmbäder eröffnet.
They have opened public pools.

430. Nachbarschaft = Neighborhood

Wir leben in einer sehr ruhigen Nachbarschaft.
We live in a very quiet neighborhood.

431. Beliebte Nachbarschaft = Popular neighborhood

Mario lebt in einer beliebten Nachbarschaft.
Mario lives in a popular neighborhood.

432. Wohngegend = Residential neighborhood

Du wohnst gut in dieser Wohngegend.
You live well in this residential neighborhood.

433. Polizeipräsidium = Police office

Geh zum Polizeipräsidium, wenn du musst.
If you need, go to the police office.

434. Postamt = Post office

Ich muss zum Postamt gehen, um ein Paket zu verschicken.
I need to go to the post office to send a package.

435. Straße = Street

Die Straßen von Altstädten sind eng.
The streets of old cities are narrow.

436. Busbahnhof = Bus station

Der Busbahnhof ist zwei Kilometer entfernt.
The bus station is two kilometers away.

437. Feuerwache = Fire station

Die Feuerwache ist immer einsatzbereit.
The fire station is always operational.

438. Straße = Road

Die Straße ist sehr verkehrsreich.
The road is very busy.

439. Vorort = Suburb

Jeder Vorort hat seine Probleme.
Every suburb has its problems.

440. Schule = School

Die Schulen schließen im Juni.
Schools close in June.

441. Krankenhaus = Hospital

Wo ist das nächste Krankenhaus?
Where is the nearest hospital, please?

442. Friedhof = Cemetery

Der Friedhof hat eine Winter- und eine Sommeröffnungszeit.
The cemetery has a winter and a summer opening hour.

443. Kirche = Church

Die Kirche feiert am Sonntag die heilige Messe.
The church celebrates mass on Sunday.

444. Wolkenkratzer = Skyscrapers

Das Geschäftsviertel ist voll mit Wolkenkratzern.
Business district is full of skyscrapers.

445. Zeitgenössische Gebäude = Period buildings

Die zeitgenössischen Gebäude befinden sich hauptsächlich im Stadtzentrum.
The period buildings are mainly downtown.

446. Historisches Gebäude = Historic building

Die historischen Gebäude in der Innenstadt stammen aus dem XVIII. Jahrhundert.
The historic buildings downtown are from the XVIII century.

447. Bürogebäude = Office building

Dies ist ein Bürogebäude.
This is an office building.

448. Villa = Mansion house

Mara lebt in einer Villa.
Mara lives in a mansion house.

449. Bibliothek = Library

Die Bibliothek organisiert interessante Treffen, die sich mit der Kunst beschäftigen.

The library organizes interesting meetings dedicated to art.

450. Kneipe = Bar

Ich kenne eine Kneipe in der Innenstadt.
I know a bar downtown.

451. Markt = Market

Auf dem Markt findest du oft Sonderpreise.
You often find special prices at the market.

452. Börse = Exchange

Die Börse eröffnet die Verhandlungen.
The Exchange is opening negotiations.

453. Zapfsäule = Petrol pump

Die Zapfsäule ist kaputt.
The petrol pump is broken.

454. Autowaschanlage = Car wash

Heute fahre ich zur Autowaschanlage, weil mein Auto schmutzig ist.
Today I go to the car wash because my car is filthy.

455. Café = Café

Die Cafés in der Innenstadt sind sehr elegant.
The cafés downtown are very elegant.

456. Kaffeebar = Coffee bar

Es gibt eine Kaffeebar, in die ich immer gehe.

There's a coffee bar that I always go to.

457. Einkaufszentrum = Shopping center

Es eröffnen immer mehr Einkaufszentren.
Shopping centers are opening more and more.

458. Raststätte = Service station

Die Raststätte ist 50 km von hier entfernt.
The service station is located 50 km from here.

459. Internetcafè = Internet cafè

Ich bin auf der Suche nach einem Internet-Café.
I'm looking for an internet cafe.

460. Apotheke = Pharmacy

Die Apotheke ist immer geöffnet.
The pharmacy is always open.

461. Kino = Cinema

Lasst uns heute Abend ins Kino gehen!
Let's go to the cinema this evening!

462. Psychiatrische Klinik = Psychiatric clinic

Wir müssen ihn in die psychiatrische Klinik bringen! Dort können sie ihm helfen.
We must take him to the psychiatric clinic! They can help him there.

463. Notaufnahme = Emergency room

Er leidet stark, bringen wir ihn in die Notaufnahme.
He's suffering a lot, let's take him to the emergency room.

464. Fitnessstudio = Gym

In der Umgebung gibt es viele Fitnessstudios.
You will find many gyms in the area.

465. Kinderspielplatz = Children's play area

In der Nähe des Hauses haben wir einen gut ausgestatteten Kinderspielplatz.
Near the house we have a well-equipped children's play area.

466. Bank = Bank

Die Banken sind morgens geöffnet.
Banks are open in the morning.

467. Stadion = Stadium

Im Stadion wird das Konzert stattfinden.
The stadium will host the concert.

468. Supermarkt = Supermarket

Ich gehe in den Supermarkt, um Eier zu kaufen.
I go to the supermarket to buy eggs.

469. Theater = Theater

Das Theater hat die Aufführungssaison eröffnet.
The theater has opened the season of performances.

MONEY
-
GELD

470. Geld = Money

Geld ist immer wichtig.
Money is always important.

471. Geld = Money

Immer fehlt Geld, wenn man es braucht.
Money is always missing when you need it.

472. Scheck = Check

Der Scheck ist eine Zahlungsmethode.
The check is a payment method.

473. Banknoten = Banknotes

Die Geldscheine, die du mir gegeben hast, sind gefälscht.
The banknotes you gave me are fake.

474. Wechselkurs = Exchange rate

Wie ist der heutige Wechselkurs?
What is the exchange rate today?

475. Kreditkarte = Credit card

Kann ich meine Kreditkarte benutzen?
Can I use my credit card?

476. Bankschließfach = Safe deposit box

Ich brauche ein Bankschließfach.
I need to have a safe deposit box.

477. Bargeld = Cash

Ich habe nur Bargeld dabei.
I only have cash with me.

478. Konto im roten = Account in red

Pass auf, dein Konto ist im roten Bereich.
Be careful because you have the account in red.

479. Dollar = Dollars

Es hat mich 15 Dollar gekostet.
It costed me 15 dollars.

480. Kontoauszug = Bank statement

Mein Kontoauszug ist online.
My bank statement is online.

481. Euro = Euro

Der Wert des Euro ist heute gestiegen.
The value of the euro has increased today.

482. Preis = Price

Der Preis hängt von der Nachfrage ab.
Price varies according to demand.

483. Rest = Rest

Hier ist der Rest.
Here you are, the rest.

484. Kontostand = Balance

Ich überprüfe meinen Kontostand.
I'm checking my balance.

485. **Pfund = Pound**

Der Pfund ist eine starke Währung.
The pound is a strong currency.

486. **Wechselkurs = Exchange rate**

Weißt du den Wechselkurs?
Do you know the exchange rate?

487. **Währung = Currency**

Die Währung ist die vom 31. Juli.
The currency is that of July 31st.

488. **Überweisung = Transfer**

Schick mir eine Überweisung auf diese IBAN.
Send me a transfer to this IBAN.

489. **Geldbörse = Wallet**

Marta hat ihre Geldbörse verloren.
Marta has lost her wallet.

490. **Die Karte aufheben = To pick up the card**

Du kannst die Karte abholen. Die Operation ist beendet.
You can pick up the card. The operation is over.

491. **Hinterlegen = To deposit**

Ich möchte Gegenstände in meinem Tresorfach hinterlegen.

I would like to deposit objects in my safe deposit box.

492. Einen Scheck ausstellen = To give a check

Ich habe kein Bargeld; kann ich dir einen Scheck ausstellen?
I don't have any cash; can I give you a check?

493. Die PIN eingeben = To enter the PIN

Bitte geben Sie Ihre PIN ein.
Please enter your PIN.

494. Abheben = To withdraw

Ich muss jetzt abheben.
I must withdraw right now.

FARBEN
-
COLOURS

495. Weiß = White

Milch ist weiß.
Milk is white.

496. Schwarz = Black

Mein Hund ist schwarz.
My dog is black.

497. Gelb = Yellow

Für Kinder ist die Sonne gelb.
The sun is yellow for children.

498. Blau = Blue

Das Meer ist blau.
The sea is blue.

499. Grün = Green

Das Gras ist grün.
The grass is green.

500. Lila = Purple

Bei Sonnenuntergang wird der Himmel violett.
At sunset, the sky becomes purple.

501. Orange = Orange

Die Karotte ist orange.
The carrot is orange.

502. Hellblau = Light blue

Der Himmel ist heute hellblau.
The sky is light blue today.

503. Rosa = Pink

Die Decke meiner Tochter ist rosa.
My daughter's blanket is pink.

504. Grau = Grey

Rauch ist grau.
Smoke is grey.

505. Rot = Red

Ich mag Rotwein
I like red wine.

506. Dunkelrot = Dark red

Der Samt war dunkelrot.
The velvet was dark red.

507. Silber = Silver

Alte Damen haben silberne Haare.
Old ladies have silver hair.

508. Elfenbeinfarben = Ivory

Elfenbeinfarben ist ein weißer Farbton.
Ivory is a white shade.

509. Gold = Gold

Gold ist eine Farbe, die Reichtum repräsentiert.
Gold is a colour that represents wealth.

510. Beige = Beige

Ich möchte ein beige-farbenes Sofa.
I want a beige-colored sofa.

511. Fuchsia = Fuchsia

Wenn du es wagen willst, entscheide dich für Fuchsia.
If you want to dare, choose fuchsia.

512. Khaki = Khaki

In diesem Jahr ist die Khaki-Farbe sehr angesagt.
This year the khaki color is very fashionable.

513. Flieder = Lilac

Du kannst diese Wand in Flieder streichen.
You can paint this wall in a lilac color.

514. Braun = Brown

Kastanien sind braun.
Chestnuts are brown.

FOOD AND RESTORATION
-
LEBENSMITTEL

515. Wasser = Water

Ich hätte gerne ein stilles Wasser.
I would like a still water.

516. Alkoholische Getränke = Alcoholic beverages

Minderjährige können keine alkoholischen Getränke kaufen.
Minors can't purchase alcoholic beverages.

517. Bier = Beer

Ich liebe alle Arten von Bier.
I love all kinds of beer.

518. Wein = Wine

Ich liebe Weißwein.
I love white wine.

519. Spirituosen = Liquor

Ich trinke nicht viel Spirituosen; ich entspanne mich lieber bei einem guten Wein.
I don't drink a lot of liquors; I'd rather relax with a good wine.

520. Absinth = Absinthe

Beim Mittagessen trinke ich lieber Absinth.
At lunch I prefer drinking absinthe.

521. Selbstgebrautes = Home Brew

Peter hat etwas Selbstgebrautes gemacht.
Peter made some home brew.

522. Doppelmalzbier = Double malt beer

Mein Lieblingsgetränk ist Doppelmalzbier.
My favorite drink is double malt beer.

523. Tonic-Wasser = Tonic water

Meine Großmutter hat das Tonic Wasser schon immer geliebt.
My grandmother has always loved tonic water.

524. Orangensaft = Orange juice

Zum Geburtstag meines Cousins habe ich sechs Flaschen Orangensaft mitgebracht.
At my cousin's birthday, I brought 6 bottles of orange juice.

525. Erfrischungsgetränke = Soft drinks

Minderjährige können Erfrischungsgetränke bestellen.
Minors can order soft drinks.

526. Energy-Drinks = Energy drink

Vor den Spielen trinke ich immer Energy-Drinks.
I always drink energy drinks before the games.

527. Alkoholfreies Bier = Alcohol-free beer

Bob trinkt alkoholfreies Bier.

Bob drinks alcohol-free beer.

528. Kaffee = Coffee

Nach dem Mittagessen ist der Kaffee für meine Familie heilig.
After lunch, coffee is sacred for my family.

529. Entkoffeiniert = Decaf

Jenny trinkt nur entkoffeinierten Kaffee.
Jenny only drinks decaf.

530. Espresso = Espresso

Sarah trank einen Espresso.
Sarah drank an espresso.

531. Geschüttelter Kaffee = Shaken coffee

Mein Onkel Gianni trinkt nur geschüttelten Kaffee.
My uncle Gianni drinks only shaken coffee.

532. Cappuccino = Cappuccino

Mein Onkel ist ein Meister im Zubereiten von Cappuccinos.
My uncle is a phenomenon at making cappuccinos.

533. Milchshake = Milkshake

Meine Freunde trinken jeden Abend einen Milchshake.
My friends have a milkshake every night.

534. Limonade = Lemonade

Limonade ist eine Delikatesse.
Lemonade is a delicacy.

535. Fruchtsäfte = Fruit Juices

Ich liebe Fruchtsäfte!
I love fruit juices!

536. Kräutertee = Herbal tea

Im Winter trinke ich vor dem Schlafengehen immer einen Kräutertee.
In winter I always take an herbal tea before sleeping.

537. Schwarzkirsche = Black cherry

Schwarzkirsche ist der Kirsche sehr ähnlich.
Black cherry is very similar to cherry.

538. Wassermelone = Watermelon

Die Wassermelone enthält viel Wasser.
Watermelon contains a lot of water.

539. Aprikose = Apricot

Die Aprikose ist Marcos Lieblingsfrucht.
Apricot is Marco's favorite fruit.

540. Orange = Orange

Orangensaft ist sehr gesund.
Orange juice is very healthy.

541. Avocado = Avocado

Avocados haben einen besonderen Geschmack, den nicht jeder mag.
The avocado has a particular taste that not everyone likes.

542. Banane = Banana

In der Küche steht ein Korb mit Bananen.
In the kitchen there is a basket of bananas.

543. Kirsche = Cherry

Meine Großmutter machte immer Kirschmarmelade.
My grandmother always made cherry jam.

544. Feigen = Fig

Martina hat gestern einen Feigenkuchen gebacken.
Martina made a fig cake yesterday.

545. Erdbeeren = Strawberries

Paolo mag Risotto mit Erdbeeren sehr gerne.
Paolo likes risotto with strawberries a lot.

546. Kiwi = Kiwi

Kinder lieben Kiwis besonders.
Children love kiwi a lot.

547. Himbeere = Raspberry

Die Himbeere ist rot.
The raspberry is red.

548. Zitrone = Lemon

Viele Cocktails beinhalten Zitronen.
Many cocktails involve the use of lemon.

549. Mandarine = Mandarin

Die Mandarine ist eine Winterfrucht.
Mandarin is a winter fruit.

550. Mango = Mango

Mangos enthalten viele Zucker.
Mango contains many sugars.

551. Apfel = Apple

Der Apfel liegt auf dem Tisch.
The apple is on the table.

552. Blaubeere = Blueberry

Die Blaubeere färbt auf Kleidung ab.
The blueberry stains clothes.

553. Brombeere = Blackberry

Die Brombeere ist schwarz.
The blackberry is black.

554. Mispel = Medlar

Die Mispel ist der Aprikose im Aussehen ähnlich.
The medlar is aesthetically similar to apricot.

555. Papaya = Papaya

Die Papaya ist eine typische exotische Frucht.
Papaya is a typical exotic fruit.

556. Birne = Pear

Die Birne ist gelb.
The pear is yellow.

557. Pfirsich = Peach

Viele junge Menschen lieben Pfirsiche.
Many young people love peaches.

558. Pflaume = Prune

Luca liebt Pflaumen.
Luca is fond of prunes.

559. Radieschen = Radish

Das Radieschen ist rot.
The radish is red.

560. Rübe = Beet

Die Zuckerrübe wird oft in Geographiebüchern erwähnt.
Sugar beet is often mentioned in geography books.

561. Karotte = Carrot

Hasen sind gierig nach Karotten.
Rabbits are greedy for carrots.

562. Blumenkohl = Cauliflower

Blumenkohl ist grün.
Cauliflower is green.

563. Zwiebel = Onion

Zwiebeln bringen die Augen zum Tränen, wenn sie roh geschnitten werden.
Onion makes your eyes water if cut raw.

564. Bohnen = Beans

Morgen werde ich Bohnen essen.
Tomorrow I will eat beans.

565. Salat = Salad

Oft Salat zu essen ist gut für die Gesundheit.
Eating salad often is good for your health.

566. Kopfsalat = Lettuce

Schnecken lieben Kopfsalat.
Snails love lettuce.

567. Linsen = Lentils

Am 31. Januar ist es in Italien sehr üblich, Linsen zu essen.
On January 31, in Italy it is very common to eat lentils.

568. Aubergine = Aubergine

Parmigiana wird mit Auberginen hergestellt.
Parmigiana is made with aubergines.

569. Melone = Melon

Es gibt verschiedene Arten von Melonen.
There are different types of melon.

570. Oregano = Oregano

Oregano ist ein in der Küche weit verbreitetes Gewürz.
Oregano is a spice widely used in cooking.

571. Gemüse = Vegetable

Gemüse ist sehr gesund.
Vegetables are very healthy.

572. Kartoffel = Potato

Die Kartoffel wächst unter der Erde.
The potato grows underground.

573. Paprika = Pepper

Marco macht oft gegrillte Paprika.
Marco often cooks grilled peppers.

574. Erbsen = Peas

Erbsen sind bei Kindern sehr beliebt.
Peas are very popular with children.

575. Tomate = Tomato

Die Soße wird aus Tomaten hergestellt.
The sauce is made with tomatoes.

576. Sellerie = Celery

Sellerie wird zur Herstellung von Gemüsesuppe verwendet.
Celery is used to make vegetable soup.

577. Spinat = Spinach

Popeye hat oft Spinat gegessen.
Popeye often ate spinach.

578. Kürbis = Pumpkin

Ende Oktober steigen die Verkaufszahlen von Kürbissen.
Pumpkin sales increase at the end of October.

579. Zucchini = Zucchini

Gestern Abend habe ich ein paar Zucchini gegessen.
Last night I ate some zucchini.

580. Pilze = Mushrooms

In den Wäldern kann man viele Pilze finden.
In the woods you can find many mushrooms.

581. Essig = Vinegard

Ich liebe Balsamico-Essig.
I love the balsamic vinegard.

582. Lamm = Lamb

Am Ostersonntag essen wir immer Lamm.
On Easter day, we always eat lamb.

583. Fleisch = Meat

Ich mag kein Fleisch.
I don't like meat.

584. Schokolade = Chocolate

Ich liebe dunkle Schokolade.
I love dark chocolate.

585. Sahne = Cream

Eine sehr geschmackvolle Sahne.
A very tasteful cream.

586. Süß = Sweet

Kartoffeln können süß sein.
Potatos can be sweet.

587. Erdbeere = Strawberry

Ich werde nur eine Erdbeere essen.
I'll eat just one strawberry.

588. Früchte = Fruits

Ich liebe alle Arten von Früchten.
I love all kind of fruits.

589. Eiscreme = Ice-cream

Das Baby liebt Eiscreme.
The baby loves ice-cream.

590. Vollkorn = Integral

Ich mag Vollkornkekse.
I like integral biscuits.

591. Milch = Milk

Ich bin allergisch gegen Milch.
I'm allergic to milk.

592. Hülsenfrüchte = Legumes

Esst Hülsenfrüchte, sie sind gesund!
Eat legumes, they're healthy!

593. Rindfleisch = Beef

Ich mag kein Rindfleisch.
I don't like beef.

594. Öl = Oil

Ich liebe Olivenöl.
I love olive oil.

595. Knochen = Bones

Ich überlasse die Knochen meinen Hunden.
I leave bones to my dogs.

596. Brot = Bread

Das Brot ist frisch.
The bread is fresh.

597. Schlagsahne = Whipped cream

Ich liebe Erdbeeren mit Schlagsahne.
I love strawberries with whipped cream.

598. Pasta = Pasta

Die Pasta ist fantastisch.
Pasta is amazing.

599. Gebäck = Pastry

Nach dem Kaffee ein Stück Gebäck.
After the coffee, a bit of pastry.

600. Kartoffel = Potato

Diese Suppe ist eine Kartoffelcremesuppe.
This soup is a potato cream.

601. Pfeffer = Pepper

Kein Pfeffer für mich.
No pepper for me.

602. Meeresfrüchte = Seafood

Was sind die heutigen Meeresfrüchte?
What is the seafood for today?

603. Fisch = Fish

Fisch passt perfekt zu Weißwein.
Fish is perfect with white wine.

604. Brust = Breast

Diese Hühnerbrust ist köstlich.
This chicken breast is delicious.

605. Pizza = Pizza

Ich liebe es, am Sonntag Pizza zu essen.
I love to eat pizza on Sunday.

606. Hühnchen = Chicken

Ich liebe Hühnchen.
I love chicken.

607. Reis = Rice

Der Reis kocht.
The rice is boiling.

608. Gesalzen = Salted

Der Fisch muss gesalzen werden.
The fish must be salted.

609. Salz = Salt

Du musst das Salz hinzugeben.
You need to add the salt.

610. Kuchen = Cake

Zu meinem Geburtstag backen wir einen Kuchen.
For my birthday we'll make a cake.

611. Ei = Egg

Nur ein Ei hier im Land?
Only one egg here in the country?

612. Gemüse = Vegetables

Ich liebe Gemüse.
I love vegetables.

613. Suppe = Soup

Ich liebe heiße Suppe.
I love hot soup.

614. Kunde = client

Paolo spricht mit einem Kunden.
Paolo is talking to a client.

615. Kocher = Cooker

Der Kocher ist erstaunlich.
The cooker is amazing.

616. Kellnerin = Waitress

Ich arbeitete als Kellnerin in einem Pub.
I worked as a waitress in a pub.

617. Koch = Chef

Wer ist deiner Meinung nach der beste Koch?
Who do you think is the best chef?

618. Pizzabäcker = Pizza maker

Ich suche einen erfahrenen Pizzabäcker.
I'm looking for an expert pizza maker.

619. Barkeeper = Barman

Barkeeper, können Sie mir bitte einen Mojito machen?
Barman, can you make me a mojito please?

620. Konditor = Pastry-cook

Wenn ich ein Konditor wäre, würde ich alle Kuchen essen.
If I was a pastry-cook, I'd eat all the cakes.

621. Bäcker = Baker

Der Bäcker arbeitet normalerweise in der Nacht.
The baker usually works at night.

622. Eismann = Ice-cream man

Ich habe einen netten Eismann kennen gelernt.
I've met a nice ice-cream man.

623. Metzger = Butcher

Der Metzger hat Qualitätsfleisch.
The butcher has quality meat.

624. Sommelier = Sommelier

In diesem Restaurant gibt es einen Sommelier.
In this restaurant there is a sommelier.

625. Restaurantkritiker = Food critic

Giovanni ist ein bekannter Restaurantkritiker.
Giovanni is a famous food critic.

626. Restaurant = Restaurant

Das Restaurant ist täglich geöffnet.
The restaurant is open every day.

627. Rechnung = Bill

Kann ich bitte die Rechnung haben?
May I have the bill please?

628. Schürze = Apron

Die Schürze darf nicht verschmutzt werden.
The apron is necessary to not get dirty.

629. Speisekarte = Menu

Kannst du mir die Speisekarte geben?
Can you pass me the menu?

630. Service = Service

Der Service war nicht gut.
The service wasn't good.

631. Gericht des Tages = Dish of the day

Das Gericht des Tages wird vom Koch ausgewählt.
The dish of the day is chosen by the chef.

632. Mexikanische Küche = Mexican cuisine

Die mexikanische Küche ist berühmt für Tacos.
The Mexican cuisine is famous for tacos.

633. Vegane Küche = Vegan cuisine

In der veganen Küche werden nur pflanzliche Zutaten verwendet.
Vegan cuisine uses only vegetables ingredients.

634. Vegetarische Küche = Vegetarian cuisine

Die vegetarische Küche ist gesund.
Vegetarian cuisine is healthy.

635. Thailändische Küche = Thai cuisine

Die thailändische Küche ist scharf.
Thai cuisine is spicy.

636. Japanische Küche = Japanese cuisine

Ein typisches Gericht der japanischen Küche ist Ramen.
A typical dish of Japanese cuisine is ramen.

637. Chinesische Küche = Chinese cuisine

Die chinesische Küche ist weltweit bekannt.
Chinese cuisine is worldwide famous.

638. Glutenfreie Küche = Gluten-free cuisine

Die glutenfreie Küche ist für Zöliakiebetroffene.

Gluten-free cuisine is for celiacs.

639. Italieniesche Küche = Italian cuisine

Das bekannteste Gericht der italienischen Küche ist die Pizza.
The most famous dish of Italian cuisine is pizza.

640. Essen = To eat

Maria isst sehr viel Pasta.
Maria eats a lot of pasta.

641. Trinken = To drink

Luigi trinkt ein Glas Wasser.
Luigi is drinking a glass of water.

642. Probieren = To taste

Luigi probiert gerne neue Lebensmittel aus.
Luigi likes tasting new foods.

643. Genießen = To savor

Ich möchte diesen Wein genießen.
I want to savor this wine.

644. Decken = To set

Luigi deckt jeden Abend den Tisch.
Luigi sets the table every evening.

645. Servieren = To serve

Gianni serviert als Kellner.
Gianni serves as waiter.

HOUSE
-
ZUHAUSE

646. Wohnung = Flat

Wir wohnen in einer Wohnung in der Stadt.
We live in a flat in the city.

647. Villa = Villa

Ich wohne lieber in einer Villa auf dem Land.
I prefer living in a country villa.

648. Doppelhaushälften = Semi-detached houses

Die Doppelhaushälften sind für uns die perfekte Lösung.
Sie geben uns ein Gefühl von Sicherheit.
The semi-detached houses are the perfect solution for us.
They give us a sense of security.

649. Studio = Studio

Ich lebe in einem Studio, weil ich allein bin.
I live in a studio because I'm alone.

650. Dachboden = Attic

Franco hat beschlossen, auf einem Dachboden zu leben.
Franco has decided to live in an attic.

651. Sozialwohnung = Council house

Diese Nachbarschaft ist voll von Sozialwohnungen.
This neighborhood is full of council houses.

652. Landhaus = Country house

Meine Familie hat ein Landhaus.
My family has a contry house.

653. Burg = Castle

In der Ferne können wir die Burg sehen.
We can see the castle in the distance.

654. Zwei-Zimmer-Wohnung = Two-room apartment

Ich lebe in einer Zwei-Zimmer-Wohnung.
I live in a two-room apartment.

655. Trullo = Trullo

In Apulien gibt es viele Trulli.
In Apulia there are many trulli.

656. Badezimmer = Bathroom

Ich gehe ins Badezimmer.
I go to the bathroom.

657. Kinderzimmer = Children room

Das Kinderzimmer ist voll von Puppen.
The children room is full of puppets.

658. Schlafzimmer = Bedroom

Mario schläft im Schlafzimmer.
Mario is sleeping in the bedroom.

659. Küche = Kitchen

Die Küche ist mein Reich.
The kitchen is my kingdom.

660. Dach = Roof

Wir müssen das Dach reparieren.
We need to repair the roof.

661. Waschküche = Laundry room

Eine Waschküche zu haben, ist sehr nützlich.
Having a laundry room is very useful.

662. Treppe = Stair

Geh die Treppe hinauf und du findest das Badezimmer.
Go up the stairs and you will find the bathroom.

663. Taverne = Tavern
Wir verbringen viele fröhliche Abende in der Taverne mit unseren Freunden
We spend many cheerfully evenings in the tavern with our friends.

664. Wohnzimmer = Living room

Wir verbringen viele Abende im Wohnzimmer.
We spend many evenings in the living room.

665. Eingang = Entry

Ich habe den Mantel am Eingang gelassen.
I left the coat at the entry.

666. Studio = Studio

Ich gehe ins Studio, um die Post zu verschicken.
I'm going to the studio to send the mail.

667. Garten = Garden

Lass uns in den Garten gehen.
Let's go to the garden.

668. Hintergarten = Back garden

Ich bin im Hintergarten.
I'm in the back garden.

669. Garage = Garage

Maria ist in der Garage zum Putzen.
Maria is in the garage to cleaning.

670. Balkon = Balcony

Der Balkon ist breit, und im Sommer sollte es schön sein, die Abende hier zu verbringen.
The balcony is wide, and, during summer, it should be nice spending the evenings here.

671. Gästezimmer = Guest room

Du wirst im Gästezimmer schlafen.
You will sleep in the guest room.

672. Esszimmer = Dining room

Heute werden wir im Esszimmer zu Mittag essen.

Today we'll have lunch in the dining room.

673. Toilette = Toilet

Die Toilette ist neu.
The toilet is new.

674. Bidet = Bidet

Wir haben das Bidet aufgestellt.
We've put the bidet.

675. Dusche = Shower

Die Dusche ging gestern kaputt.
The shower broke yesterday.

676. Wanne = Tub

Ich bevorzuge die Wanne.
I prefer the tub.

677. Waage = Scale

Die Waage befindet sich im Badezimmer.
The scale is in the bathroom.

678. Bademantel = Bathrobe

Du kannst meinen Bademantel benutzen, wenn du willst.
You can use my bathrobe if you want.

679. Toilettenpapier = Toilet paper

Das Toilettenpapier ist im Schrank.

The toilet paper is in the closet.

680. Waschbecken = Washbasin

Kannst du das Waschbecken reinigen?
Could you clean the washbasin?

681. Wasserhahn = Tap

Schließ den Wasserhahn!
Close the tap!

682. Badewanne = Bathtub

Irene, lass die Badewanne einlaufen.
Irene, fill the bathtub.

683. Badetuch = Bath towel

Hol dir ein sauberes Badetuch.
Get a clean bath towel.

684. Wecker = Alarm clock

Ich stelle meinen Wecker immer auf den Morgen.
I always set my alarm clock on morning.

685. Matratze = Mattress

ch habe eine orthopädische Matratze.
I've an orthopedic mattress.

686. Garderobe = Wardrobe

Wenn ich in meine Garderobe schauen muss, werde ich nie etwas finden. Ich besitze viele Sachen!
If I have to look into my wardrobe, I will never find anything. I own a lot of things!

687. Korb = Basket

Der Korb auf dem Schreibtisch ist voll mit Spielzeug.
The basket on the desk is full of toys.

688. Kommode = Dresser

Wir haben eine weitere Kommode gekauft.
We bought another dresser.

689. Bett = Bed

Das Bett ist sehr bequem.
The bed is very comfortable.

690. Kissen = Pillow

Dieses Kissen ist niedrig.
This pillow is low.

691. Tagesdecke = Cover

Die hellblaue Tagesdecke ist schmutzig.
The light blue cover is dirty.

692. Laken = Sheet

Das Laken auf dem Nachttisch ist für dein Bett.
The sheet on the bedside table is for your bed.

693. Decke = Blanket

Die Wolldecke ist im Schrank.
The wool blanket is in the closet.

694. Nachttisch = Bedside table

Wir haben zwei Nachttische im Schlafzimmer.
We have two bedside tables in the bedroom.

695. Schrank = Closet

Wir müssen einen neuen Schrank kaufen.
We have to buy a new closet.

696. Bild = Picture

Mir gefällt dieses Bild, das du gemalt hast.
I like this picture you painted.

697. Rahmen = Frame

Mario hat mir einen Rahmen gegeben.
Mario gave me a frame.

698. Bettdecke = Duvet

Heute Nacht werden wir mit der Bettdecke schlafen.
Tonight, we will sleep with the duvet.

699. Nachttischlampe = Bedside lamp

Wir müssen eine neue Nachttischlampe kaufen.
We must buy a new bedside lamp.

700. Tischdecke = Tablecloth

Die rote karierte Tischdecke ist in der Waschmaschine.
The red squares tablecloth is in the washing machine.

701. Kronleuchter = Chandelier

Was für einen schönen Kronleuchter du in der Küche hast!
What a beautiful chandelier you have in the kitchen!

702. Herd = Stove

Mach bitte den Herd aus.
Turn off the stove please.

703. Krug = Pitcher

Füll den Krug mit Wasser auf.
Fill the pitcher with water.

704. Anrichte = Sideboard

Ich bin gerade mit dem Aufräumen der Anrichte fertig geworden.
I've just finished cleaning up the sideboard.

705. Glas = Glass

Das Kristallglas ist da
The crystal glass is there.

706. Flasche = Bottle

Kann ich eine Flasche haben?
May I have a bottle?

707. Messer = Knife

Ein gut geformtes Messer ist hilfreich.
A well-shaped knife is helpful.

708. Löffel = Spoon

Für die Suppe brauchst du den Löffel.
For the soup, you need the spoon.

709. Gabel = Fork

Bitte benutze die Gabel, um Nudeln zu essen.
Please use the fork to eat pasta.

710. Teller = Dish

Bitte nimm deinen Teller mit.
Please take your dish.

711. Kühlschrank = Refrigerator

Maria hat den Kühlschrank abgetaut.
Maria has defrosted the refrigerator.

712. Serviette = Napkin

Die Serviette liegt auf dem Boden.
The napkin is on the floor.

713. Geschirrspülmaschine = Dishwasher

Ich weiß nicht, was ich ohne Geschirrspülmaschine machen würde.
I don't know what I would do without dishwasher.

714. Glas = Jar

Schau in das Glas in der Küche und du wirst etwas Geld finden.
Look in the jar in the kitchen and you'll find some money.

715. Geschirrspülmittel = Dishwashing detergent

Ich weiß nicht mehr, wo ich das Geschirrspülmittel hingestellt habe.
I don't remember where I've put the dishwashing detergent.

716. Gefrierschrank = Freezer

Ich benutze den Gefrierschrank sehr oft.
I use the freezer a lot.

717. Waschbecken = Sink

Für uns ist es sehr praktisch, ein kleines Waschbecken in der Garage zu haben.
For us, having a little sink in the garage is very useful.

718. Stuhl = Chair

Der Stuhl, auf dem du sitzt, ist neu.
The chair where you're sitting on is new.

719. Tisch = Table

Auf der Tabelle findest du alles, was du brauchst.
On the table you can find what you need.

720. Ofen = Oven

Stell den Truthahn in den Ofen.
Put the turkey in the oven.

721. Mikrowelle = Microwave

Ich koche eine Menge Dinge in der Mikrowelle.
I cook a lot of things in the microwave.

722. Pfanne = Pan

Ich habe eine neue Pfanne gekauft.
I've bought a new pan.

723. Topf = Pot

Dies ist der einzige Topf, den ich besitze.
This is the only pot I own.

724. Schneidebrett = Chopping board

Das Schneidebrett ist sehr nützlich, um Gemüse zu schneiden.
The chopping board is very useful to cut vegetables.

725. Weinglas = Wine glass

Gib mir das Weinglas.
Pass me the wine glass.

726. Mixer = Mixer

Ich benutze den Mixer täglich.
I use the mixer everyday.

727. Toaster = Toaster

Leg das Toastbrot in den Toaster.
Put the toast in the toaster.

728. Besteck = Dish set

In diesem Restaurant haben sie schönes Besteck.
In that restaurant they have a nice dish set.

729. Regal = Shelf

Ich habe ein rotes Regal im Wohnzimmer.
I've a red shelf in the living room.

730. Zimmerpflanze = Room plant

Ich habe viele Zimmerpflanzen für mein neues Haus gekauft.
I've bought many room plants for my new house.

731. Fernseher = Television

Wenn du den Fernseher einschaltest, musst du die Lautstärke niedrig halten.
If you turn on the television, keep the volume low.

732. Sofa = Sofa

Wir haben ein King-Sofa.
We have a king sofa.

733. Sessel = Armchair

Ich habe einen neuen Sessel gekauft.
I bought a new armchair.

734. Teppich = Carpet

Der rote Teppich liegt im Wohnzimmer.
The red carpet is in the living room.

735. Klimaanlage = Air conditioner

Im Sommer schalten wir die Klimaanlage ein.
On summer, we turn on the air conditioner.

736. Uhr = Clock

Die Uhr im Wohnzimmer ist im Vintage-Stil gehalten.
The living room clock is vintage style.

737. Vorhänge = Curtains

Ich habe einige gelbe Vorhänge für das Wohnzimmer gekauft.
I've bought some yellow curtains for the living room.

738. Fenster = Window

Mein Fenster zeigt auf den Innenhof.
My window faces on the courtyard.

739. Radio = Radio

Ich höre lieber Radio.
I prefer listening to the radio.

740. CD-Player = Cd player

Der CD-Player ist ein bisschen alt.
The CD player is a bit old.

741. Konsole = Console

Wenn du die Konsole einschaltest, spielen wir ein Spiel.
If you turn on the console, we'll play a game.

742. Bücherregal = Bookcase

Maras Bücherregal ist voller klassischer und moderner Bücher, denn sie liebt das Lesen.
Mara's bookcase is rich of classic and modern books because she loves reading.

743. Ventilator = Fan

Der Ventilator reicht aus.
The fan is enough.

744. Kamin = Fireplace

Im Winter lassen wir oft den Kamin angezündet, um das Haus zu heizen und eine besondere Atmosphäre zu schaffen.
On winter, we often keep the fireplace lit to heat the house and give a certain atmosphere.

745. Heizkörper = Radiator

Im Oktober schalten wir die Heizkörper ein.
On October, we turn on the radiators.

746. Verzierungen = Ornament

Mario hat zu viele Verzierungen im Haus.
Mario has too many ornaments in the house.

747. Schlüssel = Keys

Hast du die Hausschlüssel?
Do you have the house keys?

748. Schloss = Lock

Mein Schloss hat sich verhakt, und deshalb muss ich einen Schlosser anrufen, um es zu reparieren.
My lock got stuck and because of this, I need to call a smith to fix it.

749. Tür = Door

Die Tür ist offen.
The door is open.

750. Schuhregal = Shoe rack

Pack deine Hausschuhe in das Schuhregal.
Put your slippers in the shoe rack.

751. Kleiderständer = Hall stand

Ich habe deine Jacke am Kleiderständer in der Halle am Eingang aufgehängt. Wenn du rausgehst, kannst du sie da finden.
I hung up your jacket in the hall stand at the entrance. When you go out, you can find it there.

752. Sicherheitstür = Security door

In der Stadt ist eine Sicherheitstür unerlässlich.
In the city, the security door is essential.

753. Schwamm = Sponge

Der grüne Schwamm ist für die Küche.
The green sponge is for the kitchen.

754. Kessel = Boiler

Der Kessel ist kaputt gegangen.
The boiler broke down.

755. Waschmaschine = Washing machine

Maria hat aus Bequemlichkeit zwei Waschmaschinen.
Maria has two washing machines for convenience.

756. Trockner = Dryer

Der Trockner erlaubt es dir, deine Kleidung zu trocknen, ohne sie herauszuhängen.

The dryer allows you to dry your clothes without hanging them out.

757. Teppichboden = Floor cloth

Ich gehe jeden Morgen über den Teppichboden.
I pass the floor cloth every morning.

758. Staubsauger = Vacuum cleaner

Wenn mein Staubsauger kaputt geht, bin ich erledigt!

If my vacuum cleaner breaks, I'm ruined!

759. Bügeleisen = Iron

Unser Bügeleisen ist unbenutzt.
Our iron is unused.

760. Besen = Broom

Kannst du mir den Besen geben?
Can you give me the broom?

761. Scheuerbürste = Scrubbing brush

Die Scheuerbürste findest du im Lagerraum.
You can find the scrubbing brush in the storage room.

762. Haupttür = Main door

Wer schlägt immer die Haupttür zu?
Who always slams the main door?

763. Fußmatte = Door mat

Mach Deine Füße auf der Türmatte sauber.
Clean your feet on the door mat.

764. Regenschirmständer = Umbrella stand

Stelle den Regenschirm in den Regenschirmständer.
Put the ubrella in the umbrella stand.

765. Sicherheitsalarm = Security alarm

Stell den Sicherheitsalarm ein.

Turn on the security alarm.

766. Aufzug = Elevator

Ich wohne in der 8. Etage. Was würde ich ohne den Aufzug machen?
I live at the 8th floor. What would I do without the elevator?

767. Aschenbecher = Ashtray

Hast du bitte einen Aschenbecher?
Do you have an ashtray please?

768. Pott = Pot

Mir gefallen die Pötte, die du für die Balkonpflanzen ausgewählt hast.
I like the pots that you chose for the balcony plants.

769. Hundehütte = Dog house

Die Hundehütte befindet sich im Garten.
The doghouse is in the garden.

770. Blumenbeet = Flower bed

Das Blumenbeet ist voller farbenfroher Blumen.
That flower bed is full of colorful flowers.

771. Gießkanne = Watering can

Wenn du mir die Gießkanne bringst, kümmere ich mich um die Bewässerung der Pflanzen.

If you bring me the watering can, I'll take care of watering plants.

772. Axt = Axe

Nimm bitte eine Axt.
Take an axe please.

773. Tor = Gate

Das Tor ist kaputt, du musst das Schloss austauschen.
The gate is broken, you need to change the lock.

774. Schuppen = Shed

Ich habe einen Schuppen voll mit Werkzeugen.
I have a shed full of tools.

775. Schubkarre = Wheelbarrow

Frag den Nachbarn nach einer Schubkarre, damit wir diese Blätter schneller in den Mülleimer werfen können.
Ask the neighbour a wheelbarrow so we can transfer these leaves to the dustbin more quickly.

776. Briefkasten = Letterbox

Im Briefkasten findest du meine Nachricht.
In the letterbox you will find my message.

777. Gartenschere = Secateurs

Wenn du diese Hecken gut trimmen willst, musst du eine Gartenschere kaufen, sonst wird das nicht klappen.

If you want to trim well these hedges, you need to buy secateurs otherwise you won't do it.

778. Mülltonne = Dustbin

Die Mülltonne muss entleert werden, da sie stinkt.
The dustbin must be emptied because it stinks.

779. Heugabel = Fork

Wir brauchen eine Heugabel, um das ganze Heu zu bewegen.
We need the fork to move all this hay.

780. Kies = Gravel

Ich möchte bei der Einfahrt etwas Kies haben.
I want some gravel in the entry drive.

781. Harke = Rake

Wo haben wir die Harke hingestellt?
Where did we put the rake?

782. Treibhaus = Greenhouse

In meinem Gewächshaus habe ich viele Zitronen.
In my greenhouse I have many lemons.

783. Zaun = Fence

Der Zaun muss komplett neu gestrichen werden.
The fence needs to be completely repainted.

784. Rasenmäher = Lawn-mower

Er hat den Rasenmäher zwei Stunden lang benutzt.
He has been using the lawn-mower for two hours.

785. Spaten = Spade

Der Spaten ist ideal, um dieses Loch zu graben.
The spade is ideal to dig this hole.

786. Blumenpott = Flowerpot

Mario kaufte einen neuen Blumenpott und stellte ihn in das Wohnzimmer.
Mario bought a new flowerpot and he put it in the living room.

787. Einfahrt = Drive

Die Einfahrt führt zum Mücheneingang.
The drive leads to the kitchen entry.

788. Hacke = Hoe

Luigi hat eine neue Hacke.
Luigi has a new hoe.

789. Hausarbeit = Housework

Ich hasse es, Hausarbeit zu machen!
I hate doing housework!

790. Rechnungen = Bills

Jeden Monat müssen Rechnungen bezahlt werden.

Every month there are bills to pay.

791. Mietgebühren = Condo fees

Die Mietgebühren müssen bezahlt werden, um rechtliche Probleme zu vermeiden.
The condo fees must be paid to avoid legal issues.

792. Architekt = Architect

Für deine Wohnung brauchst du einen Architekten.
You need an architect for your flat.

793. Verwalter = Administrator

Ich werde den Verwalter für Informationen anrufen.
I will call the administrator for information.

794. Hausfrau = Housewife

Meine Mutter ist eine Hausfrau.
My mother is a housewife.

795. Bauherr = Builder

Der Bauherr griff in die Arbeiten ein.
The builder intervened in the work.

796. Immobilienmakler = Real estate agent

Mara rief einen Immobilienmakler an, um ihr Haus zu verkaufen.
Mara called a real estate agent to sell her house.

797. Inneneinrichtung = Interior design

Ich habe 3 Jahre lang Innenarchitektur studiert.
I've studied interior design for 3 years.

798. Restaurator = Restorer

Mein Vater ist ein Restaurator.
My dad is a restorer.

799. Leben = To live

Wir leben in Rom.
We live in Rome.

800. Leben = To live

Ich lebe in Mailand.
I live in Milan.

801. Mieten = To rent

Sie mieten ihre Wohnung.
They rent their flat.

ABOUT SHOPPING
-
ÜBER DAS EINKAUFEN

802. Socken = Sock

Ich habe einen Socken verloren.
I've lost a sock.

803. Strumpfhosen = Tights

Strumpfhosen sind sehr anfällig.
Tights are very fragile.

804. Hut = Hat

Ich liebe den grünen Hut.
I love the green hat.

805. Mantel = Coat

Ich liebe deinen schwarzen Mantel.
I love your black coat.

806. Krawatte = Tie

Es ist besser, im Büro eine Krawatte zu tragen.
In the office it's better to wear a tie.

807. Jacke = Jacket

Meine Jacke ist handgefertigt.
My jacket is handmade.

808. Pelzmantel = Fur coat

Dieser Pelzmantel ist übertrieben.
That fur coat is excessive.

809. Bademantel = Dressing gown

Meine Großmutter trägt immer einen Bademantel.
My grandmother always wears a dressing gown.

810. Schlafanzug = Nightgown

Ich trage zum Schlafen immer einen Schlafanzug.
I always wear a nightgown to sleep.

811. Rock = Skirt

Du hast einen schönen Rock an.
You're wearing a nice skirt.

812. Hemd = Shirt

Ich liebe das rote Hemd.
I love the red shirt.

813. T-Shirt = T-shirt

Ich habe kein T-Shirt mehr übrig.
I have no more t-shirt left.

814. Brille = Glasses

Ich trage immer eine Brille.
I always wear glasses.

815. Hose = Trousers

Ich liebe deine weiße Hose.
I love your white trousers.

816. Schuhe = Shoes

Ich habe nur noch zwei Schuhe.
I have only two shoes left.

817. Stiefel = Boots

Meine Schneestiefel sind kaputt.
My snow boots are broken.

818. Schal = Scarf

Hast du den Winterschal gekauft?
Did you buy the winter scarf?

819. Klammern = Braces

Ich denke, Klammern sind dumm.
I think braces are stupid.

820. Regenschirm = Umbrella

Auch wenn es nicht regnet, habe ich immer einen Regenschirm dabei.
Even if it's not raining, I always carry an umbrella.

821. Handschuhe = Gloves

Mein Fahrer trägt oft Handschuhe.
My driver often wears gloves.

822. Tasche = Bag

Ich möchte eine Gucci-Tasche.
I want a Gucci bag.

823. High Heels = High heels

Du trägst oft High Heels.
You often wear high heels.

824. Anzug = Suit

Ich habe einen sehr eleganten Anzug gekauft.
I bought a very elegant suit.

825. Ring = Ring

Hier ist mein Verlobungsring.
Here's my engagement ring.

826. Armband = Bracelet

Das Armband von Mara ist aus Gold.
Mara's bracelet is in gold.

827. Hemd = Shirt

Das Hemd von Marco hat Flecken.
Marco's shirt is stained.

828. Bluse = Blouse

Diese seidene Frauenbluse kostet 120 Euro.
This silk woman blouse costs 120 euros.

829. Strickjacke = Cardigan

Zu diesem Rock brauchst du eine Strickjacke.
You need a cardigan on this skirt.

830. Gürtel = Belt

Ich brauche einen Gürtel für die Hose.
I need a belt for the trousers.

831. Halskette = Necklace

Die Perlenhalskette ist immer ein Klassiker.
The pearl necklace is always a classic.

832. Badehose = Swimming shorts

Luigi will eine Badehose kaufen.
Luigi wants to buy swimming shorts.

833. Uniform = Uniform

Sie müssen in diesem College eine Uniform tragen: Das ist Vorschrift!
They must wear a uniform in that college: it's a rule!

834. Sweatshirt = Sweatshirt

Ein Sweatshirt ist bei jeder Gelegenheit bequem.
A sweatshirt is comfortable in every occasion.

835. Weste = Waistcoat

Eine Weste würde dir einen kleinen Hauch von Eleganz verleihen.
A waistcoat would give you a little touch of fashion.

836. Jacke = Jacket

Mir ist kalt, kannst du mir bitte die Jacke geben?
I'm cold, can you hand me the jacket please?

837. Regenmantel = Raincoat

Der Regenmantel ist während Übergangsjahreszeiten perfekt.
The raincoat is perfect during half-seasons.

838. Flip-Flops = Flip-flop

Ich trage gerne Flip-Flops.
I love wearing flip-flops.

839. Leggings = Leggings

Ich denke, dass Leggings sehr bequem sind.
I believe that leggings are very comfortable.

840. Pullover = Pullover

Ich brauche einen Pullover.
I need a pullover.

841. Höschen oder Unterhose = Panties or Underpants

Ich muss 10 Paar Unterhosen kaufen.
I need to buy 10 pairs of panties.

842. Sonnenbrille = Sunglasses

Meine Sonnenbrille ist kaputt.
My sunglasses are broken.

843. Ohrringe = Earrings

Die Ohrringe meiner Mutter sind aus Silber.
My mom's earrings are made of silver.

844. Shorts = Shorts

Im Sommer trägt Luisa immer Shorts, weil es heiß ist und sie es hasst, Jeans zu tragen.
During summer Luisa always wears shorts because it's hot and she can't stand wearing jeans.

845. Fliege = Bow tie

Die Fliege ist ein sehr unbedarftes Accessoire.
The bow tie is a very naif accessory.

846. Schlafanzug = Pyjamas

Ich liebe bequeme Pyjamas.
I love comfortable pyjamas.

847. Polo-Shirt = Polo-shirt

Das Polo-Shirt eignet sich perfekt zum Golfspielen.
The polo-shirt is perfect to play golf.

848. BH = Bra

Ein guter BH hat eine große Wirkung.
A good bra makes a great effect.

849. Sandalen = Sandals

Sandalen sind sehr teuer.

Sandals are very expensive.

850. Hochhackige Schuhe = High-heeled shoes

Ich kann keine hochhackigen Schuhe tragen.
I'm unable to wear high-heeled shoes.

851. Turnschuhe = Sneakers

Ich trage nur Turnschuhe.
I only wear sneakers.

852. Haarklammer = Hairgrip

Kann ich mir eine Haarklammer ausleihen?
Can I borrow a hairgrip?

853. Haarband = Hair band

Ich brauche ein Haarband zum Zusammenbinden meiner Haare.
I need a hair band to tie my hair.

854. Stiefel = Boots

Die Lederstiefel werden zu einem Rabatt von 50% verkauft.
The leather boots are on sale at 50%.

855. Oberteil = Top

Das Oberteil, das du trägst, ist fantastisch!
The top you're wearing is fantastic!

856. Trainingsanzug = Tracksuit

Ein Trainingsanzug ist das ideale Geschenk.
A tracksuit is the ideal gift.

857. Kleid = Dress

Ich muss ein Kleid für die Party kaufen.
I must buy a dress for the party.

858. Stoff = Fabric

Der Stoff ist sehr weich.
The fabric is very soft.

859. Wolle = Cotton

Baumwolle ist eine Naturfaser.
Cotton is a natural fiber.

860. Spitze = Lace

Spitze wurden im letzten Jahrhundert häufig für edle Damenkleider verwendet.
The lace was used a lot in the last century for noble ladies' clothes.

861. Leinen = Linen

Leinen ist ein schwierig zu bügelnder Stoff.
Linen is a difficult fabric to iron.

862. Geschäft = Store

Hat das Geschäft geöffnet?

Is the store open?

863. Gutschein = Coupon

Ich habe keinen Gutschein.
I don't have any coupon.

864. Rabatt = Discount

Gibt es einen besonderen Rabatt?
Is there any special discount?

865. Laufsteg = Catwalk

Gestern war ich auf einem Laufsteg.
Yesterday I went to a catwalk.

866. Schaufenster = Shopping window

Schau, wie wunderbar das Schaufenster des Valentino's ist.
Look how wonderful the Valentino's shopping window is.

867. Umkleidekabine = Dressing room

Wo sind die Umkleidekabinen?
Where are the dressing rooms?

868. Umtausch = To change

Ich muss etwas umtauschen, weil das zu T-Shirt klein ist.
I need to have a change because the T-shirt is small.

869. Krücke = Crutch

Ich brauche eine Krücke, die ich in meinen Schrank stellen kann.
I need a crutch to put in my closet.

870. Modedesigner = Fashion designer

Modedesigner haben in diesem Jahr etwas übertrieben.
Fashion designers have exaggerated this year.

871. Ladenbesitzer = Shopkeeper

Franco ist seit Jahren Ladenbesitzer.
Franco has been a storekeeper for years.

872. Juwelier = Jeweler

Ich habe die Halskette bei einem Juwelier gekauft.
I bought the necklace by a jeweler.

873. Verkäufer = Shop assistant

Frag bei einem Verkäufer nach der Größe.
Ask for the size to a shop assistant.

874. Anziehen = To dress

Ich hasse es, die Puppe meiner Tochter anzuziehen.
I hate to dress my daughter's doll.

875. Nähen = To sew

Kannst du diese Hose bitte für mich nähen?
Can you sew these trousers for me, please?

BEAUTY
-
SCHÖNHEIT

876. Eyeliner = Eyeliner

Ich ziehe Eyeliner dem Kajalstift vor.
I prefer eyeliner to eye pencil.

877. Grundierung = Foundation

Im Winter färbt die Grundierung und schützt die Haut vor Schadstoffen.
During winter the foundation colours and protects the skin from pollution agents.

878. Rouge = Blush

Ich muss meine Bräune mit etwas Rouge auffrischen.
I must revive my tan with a bit of blush.

879. Lippenbalsam = Lip balm

Benutz ein Lippenbalsam, wenn deine Lippen rissig sind.
Use a lip balm when your lips are cracked.

880. Gesichtsmaske = Face mask

Heute werden im Supermarkt Gesichtsmasken angeboten.
Today, face mask on offer at the supermarket.

881. Kajalstift = Eye pencil

Ich habe einen grünen Kajalstift.
I've a green eye pencil.

882. Schminkpinsel = Make-up brush

Kannst du mir einen Schminkpinsel schenken?

Can you gift me a make-up brush?

883. Lippenstift = Lipstick

Rosa Lippenstift, über alles!
Pink lipstick, always!

884. Nagellack = Nail varnish

Wenn ich mich für einen Nagellack entscheiden muss, bevorzuge ich den transparenten.
If I must choose a nail varnish, I prefer the transparent one.

885. Gesichtsreinigung = Face cleaning

Mara macht zweimal im Jahr eine Gesichtsreinigung.
Mara does the face cleaning twice per year.

886. Frisur = Hairstyle

Sie hat eine seltsame Frisur!
She has a strange hairstyle!

887. Haarspülung = Conditioner

Wenn du möchtest, dass deine Haare schön sind, dann musst du Haarspülung nach der Haarwäsche verwenden.
If you want your hairs to be nice, use the conditioner after shampooing.

888. Lockenwickler = Curler

Wenn du mir die Lockenwickler gibst, tust du mir einen Gefallen.
If you give me the curlers, you'll do me a favor.

889. Locken = Curls

Für diesen besonderen Anlass habe ich mir Locken gemacht.
For this special occasion I made curls.

890. Kurzes Haar = Short hair

Kurzes Haar ist praktischer.
Short hair is more practical.

891. Langes Haar = Long hair

Ich bevorzuge langes Haar.
I prefer long hair.

892. Pagenkopf = Pageboy

Sie hat einen hübschen blonden Pagenkopf.
She has a nice blonde pageboy.

893. Strähnchen = Highlights

Diesen Sommer möchte ich meiner Frisur Farbe geben, und ich werde Strähnchen machen.
This summer I want to give color to my hairstyle, and I will make highlights.

894. Schere = Scissor

Maria hat eine scharfe Schere.
Maria has a sharp scissor.

895. Gel = Gel

Hast du ein bisschen Haargel?
Have you got a bit of hair gel?

896. Haarspray = Hairspray

Das Haarspray ist nützlich, um Frisuren zu fixieren.
The hairspray is useful to fix the hairstyle.

897. Haare richten = Hair set

Ich lasse mir die Haare richten.
I'm going to get a hair set.

898. Dauerwelle = Permanent wave

Es ist an der Zeit, die Dauerwelle zu erneuern.
It's time to redo the permanent wave.

899. Kamm = Comb

Der Kamm entwirrt mein Haar nach der Spülung. Das ist ein wichtiger Schritt.
The comb detangles my hair after the conditioner. This is an important operation to do.

900. Föhn = Hairdryer

Der Föhn steht im Regal.
The hairdryer is on the shelf.

901. Glätter = Straightener

Heute benutze ich keinen Haarglätter.
Today I pass the hair straightener.

902. Haarschaum = Hair foam

Wenn du lockiges Haar haben möchtest, musst du den Haarschaum verwenden.
If you want curly hair use the hair foam.

903. Shampoo = Shampoo

Das Shampoo ist in der Dusche.
Shampoo is in the shower.

904. Bürste = Brush

Kann ich deine Bürste nehmen?
Can I take your brush?

905. Schwarzes Haar = Black hair

Das Mädchen hat wunderschönes schwarzes Haar.
That girl has beautiful black hair.

906. Blondes Haar = Blonde hair

Ich möchte blondes Haar haben!
I want blonde hair!

907. Braunes Haar = Brown hair

Your friend with brown hair is cute.

908. Rotes Haar = Red hair

Ich kenne nur wenige Menschen mit roten Haaren.
I know few people with red hair.

909. Glattes Haar = Straight hair

Mit glattem Haar gefalle ich mir besser.
I like myself better with straight hair.

910. Gelocktes Haar = Curly hair

Mädchen mit gelocktem Haar sind sehr schön.
Girls with curly hair are very beautiful.

911. Gewelltes Haar = Wavy hair

Heute Abend gehe ich mit gewelltem Haar aus.
Tonight, I'm going out with wavy hair.

912. Kahl = Bald

Mein Chef hat einem kahle Kopf.
My boss is bald.

913. Nachgebender Haaransatz = Receding hairline

Dein Vater hat einen großen, nachgebenden Haaransatz.
Your dad has a big receding hairline.

914. Aftershave = After-shave

Mir gefällt das Aftershave, das du benutzt.
I like the after-shave that you use.

915. Rasierer = Razor

Dieser Rasierer ist alt.

This razor is old.

916. Rasierschaum = Shaving cream

Der Rasierschaum ist leer. Kannst du mir bitte neuen Rasierschaum kaufen, wenn du in den Supermarkt gehst?
The shaving cream is over. If you go to the supermarket, can you buy one please?

917. Binden = Pads

Eine Packung Binden, bitte.
One pack of pads, please.

918. Enthaarungswachs = Depilatory wax

Zum Rasieren bevorzuge ich ein Enthaarungswachs.
To shave myself I prefer having a depilatory wax.

919. Feuchtigkeitscreme = Moisturizing cream

Schon in jungen Jahren benötigt die Haut Feuchtigkeitscreme.
From a young age, the skin needs a moisturizing cream.

920. Deodorant = Deodorant

Mein Deodorant verursacht bei mir keine Allergien.
My deodorant doesn't cause me allergies.

921. Dusche = Shower

Das Duschgel ist bereit.
The shower gel is ready.

922. Reinigungsmilch = Cleansing milk

Entferne das Make-up mit der Reinigungsmilch.
Remove the make-up with the cleansing milk.

923. Nagelfeile = Nail file

Mein Fingernagel ist abgebrochen. Kann ich mir eine Nagelfeile leihen, damit ich ihn sofort reparieren kann?
My fingernail got broken. Can I borrow a nail file so I can fix it right now?

924. Feuchtigkeitsmaske = Hydrant mask

Eine Feuchtigkeitsmaske jeden Monat ist gut für mein Gesicht.
A hydrant mask every month is good for my face.

925. Nagellack = Nail polish

Ich brauche den Nagellack
I need the nail polish.

926. Intimreiniger = Intimate cleanser

Der Intimreiniger muss zart sein.
The intimate cleanser must be delicate.

927. Seife = Soap

Wasch deine Hände richtig mit Seife.
Wash properly your hands with soap.

928. Kosmetiker = Beautician

Heute gehe ich zur Kosmetikerin.
Today I'm going to the beautician.

929. Masseur = Masseur

Heute gehe ich zum Masseur
I go to the masseur.

930. Masseurin = Masseuse

Luisa hat eine Masseurin angerufen.
Luisa called a masseuse.

931. Visagistin = Make-up artist

Die Visagistin weiß, wie sie diese dunklen Flecken zu verbergen hat.
The make-up artist knows how to hide these dark circles.

932. Barbier = Barber

Geh zum Barbier, um dich wieder frisch zu machen.
Go to the barber to fix you up.

933. Rasieren = To shave

Du musst dich öfter rasieren.
You need to shave more often.

934. Waschen = To wash

Maria wäscht ihre Hosen.
Maria washes her trousers.

935. Kämmen = To comb

Lass uns das Baby kämmen.
Let's comb the baby.

CONVERSATION
-
KONVERSATION

936. Hallo = Hello

Hallo Marco!
Hello Marco!

937. Guten Morgen = Good morning

Guten Morgen Luca, bist du bereit?
Good morning Luca, are you ready?

938. Guten Abend = Good Evening

Guten Abend, Marisa! Ich liebe dein Kleid.
Good evening Marisa! I love your dress.

939. Willkommen = Welcome

Willkommen in diesem Haus!
Welcome in this house!

940. Gute Nacht = Good night

Gute Nacht, Mama!
Good night Mum!

941. Auf Wiedersehen = Goodbye

Auf Wiedersehen und danke für die Hilfe.
Goodbye and thanks for the help.

942. Bis bald = See you soon

Jetzt muss ich gehen. Bis bald!
Now I have to go. See you soon!

943. Bis später = See you later

Und sie sagte mir: "Bis später!"
And she told me "See you later!".

944. Bis morgen = See you tomorrow

Es ist eine fantastische Party, aber ich muss gehen. Bis morgen!
It's a fantastic party, but I have to go. See you tomorrow!

945. Wann? = When?

Wann hast du Zeit?
When are you free?

946. Was? = What?

Was machst du?
What are you doing?

947. Warum? = Why?

Warum warst du gestern Abend im Park?
Why were you at the park last night?

948. Wo? = Where?

Wo bist du?
Where are you?

949. Wer? = Who?

Wer sind diese Leute?
Who are these people?

950. Wie viel? = How much?

Wie viel kostet es?
How much is it?

951. Wie? = How?

Wie kommen wir ins Stadtzentrum?
How can we arrive to the city center?

952. Welches = Which?

Welches T-Shirt kaufst du?
Which T-shirt are you buying?

953. Ja = Yes

Ja, bis später.
Yes, see you later.

954. Natürlich! = Of course!

Mögen Sie Volleyball? Natürlich!
Do you like volleyball? Of course!

955. Nein = No

Magst du deinen Chef? Nein, ich mag ihn nicht.
Do you like your boss? No, I don't.

956. Vielleicht = Maybe

Vielleicht werde ich morgen nicht zur Arbeit gehen.
Maybe I won't go to work tomorrow.

957. Warum nicht! = Why not!

Was wäre, wenn wir eine Party schmeißen würden?
Warum nicht?
What If we threw a party? Why not?

FEELINGS AND CHARACTER

GEFÜHLE UDN CHARAKTER

958. Entschlossenheit = Determination

Sie hat die Entschlossenheit eines Löwen.
She has the determination of a lion.

959. Bewunderung = Admiration

Marco empfindet viel Bewunderung für Paul.
Marco feels a lot of admiration for Paul.

960. Liebe = Love

Marco hat sich 2014 in Marta verliebt.
Marco fell in love with Marta in 2014.

961. Angst = Anguish

John lebt in einem permanenten Zustand der Angst.
John lives in a state of anguish.

962. Mitgefühl = Compassion

Mitgefühl ist eine noble Eigenschaft.
Compassion is a noble dowry.

963. Begeisterung = Enthusiasm

Er erhielt die Nachricht mit großer Begeisterung.
He got the news with great enthusiasm.

964. Vertrauen = Trust

Vertrauen ist die Grundlage jeder Beziehung.
Trust is the base of every relationship.

965. Brüderlichkeit = Fraternity

Die Brüderlichkeit, die zwischen Marco und Roberta besteht, ist beispiellos.
The fraternity that exists between Marco and Roberta is unparalleled.

966. Frust = Frustration

Dieser Job bereitet mir viel Frust.
This job is giving me much frustration.

967. Eifersucht = Jealousy

Eifersucht ist ein schlechtes Gefühl.
Jealousy is a bad feeling.

968. Belohnung = Gratification

Ihre Freude ist meine Belohnung.
Her joy is my gratification.

969. Gleichgültigkeit = Indifference

Gleichgültigkeit ist eine Form der Gewalt.
Indiffence is a form of violence.

970. Empörung = Indignation

Das Zitat hat starke Entrüstung ausgelöst.
That quote caused strong indignation.

971. Neid = Envy

Neid ist eine Todsünde.

Envy is a cardinal sin.

972. Melancholie = Melancholy

Melancholie ist ein typisches Gefühl der romantischen Dichter.
Melancholy is a typical feeling of romantic poets.

973. Hass = Hate

Hass hat nur schlechte Auswirkungen.
Hate has only bad effects.

974. Ehre = Honor

Peep ging mit Ehre.
Peep left with honor.

975. Vergebung = Forgiveness

Gott schenkt immer seine Vergebung.
God always gives his forgiveness.

976. Wut = Anger

Wut kann in Hass umschlagen.
Anger can turn into hate.

977. Mitgefühl = Simpathy

Ich weiß sein Mitgefühl wirklich zu schätzen.
I really appreciate his simpathy.

978. Scham = Shame

Melania wurde aus Scham rot.
Melania turned red because of shame.

979. Motivation = Motivation

Martina hat eine sehr starke Motivation.
Martina has a very strong motivation.

980. Spaß = Fun

Die Schule ist auch ein Ort des Spaßes.
School is also a place for fun.

981. Langeweile = Boredom

Ich sterbe vor Langeweile.
I'm dying of boredom.

982. Respekt = Respect

Der Respekt vor anderen muss in der Schule gelehrt werden.
Respect for others must be taught at school.

983. Kreativität = Creativity

Schule fördert die Kreativität.
School stimulates creativity.

984. Ehrlichkeit = Sincerity

In einer Beziehung muss es immer Ehrlichkeit geben.
There must always be sincerity in a relationship.

985. Freude = Happiness

Ein Freund ist da, auch wenn Freude nicht da ist.
A friend is there even when happiness isn't.

986. Freundlichkeit = Kindness

Freundlichkeit wird oft für Schwäche gehalten.
The kindness is often taken for weakness.

987. Loyalität = Loyalty

In einer Freundschaft gibt es immer Loyalität.
In a friendship there is always loyalty.

TRAVEL - REISEN

988. Historisches Denkmal = Historical monument

Vor uns steht ein historisches Denkmal von großer Bedeutung.
That in front of us is an historical monument of great importance.

989. Denkmal = Monument

Jedes Denkmal hat seine Geschichte zu erzählen.
Each monument has its story to tell.

990. Museum = Museum

Die Schülerinnen und Schüler werden einen Ausflug in das ägyptische Museum unternehmen.
The students will be going on a trip to the Egyptian museum.

991. Kunstgallerie = Art gallery

Die Kunstgalerie ist ein Ort, an dem Gemälde renommierter Künstler ausgestellt werden.
The art gallery is a place where paintings of renowed artists are collected.

992. Statue = Statue

Die Statue des Helden steht auf dem Hauptplatz der Stadt.
The hero's statue is in the main square of the city.

993. Gasthaus = Guest house

Kannst du uns bitte die Liste der Gasthäuser geben?

Can you give us the guest house list, please?

994. Hotel = Hotel

Unser Hotel ist direkt vor dem Kolosseum.
Our hotel is right in front of the Colosseum.

995. Pension = Boarding house

Wir haben eine schöne und saubere Pension gefunden.
We've found a nice and clean boarding house.

996. Campen = Camping

Ich liebe Campen.
I love camping.

997. Campingzelt = Camping tent

Ich muss ein Campingzelt für diesen Sommer kaufen.
I have to buy a camping tent for this summer.

998. Wohnmobil = Camper

Mein Vater hat gerade ein neues Wohnmobil gekauft.
My dad has just bought a new camper.

999. Wohnwagen = Caravan

Ich mag Wohnwagen mehr als Wohnmobile.
I like caravans more than campers.

1000. Hütte = Cabin

In der Hütte ist es sehr kalt.

The cabin is very cold.

1001. Mit dem Flugzeug = By plane

Von Mailand nach London dauert es etwa eine Stunde und 20 Minuten mit dem Flugzeug.
From Milan to London it takes about an hour and 20 by plane.

1002. Mit dem Auto = By car

Mit dem Auto in der Innenstadt zu fahren ist schwierig.
Driving in the city centre by car is difficult.

1003. Mit dem Boot = By boat

Ein Urlaub mit dem Boot ist für diejenigen zu empfehlen, die flexibel sind.
A holiday by boat is reccomended for those who have adaptability.

1004. Mit dem Fahrrad = By bike

Es ist besser, sich in der Altstadt mit dem Fahrrad fortzubewegen.
It's better to move by bike in the historic center.

1005. Mit dem Motorrad = By motorcycle

Sie haben beschlossen, Ligurien mit dem Motorrad zu besuchen.
They have decided to visit Liguria by motorcycle.

1006. Mit dem Schiff = By ship

Sie können die Insel Giglio mit dem Schiff von Argentario aus erreichen.
You can reach Giglio island by ship from Argentario.

1007. Mit dem Bus = By bus

Du kannst das Stadtzentrum mit dem Bus erreichen.
You can reach the city center by bus.

1008. Mit dem Zug = By train

Er besuchte ganz Europa mit dem Zug.
He visited all Europe moving by train.

1009. Reiseagentur = Travel agency

Wir gehen in die Reiseagentur, um die Reise zu buchen.
We go to the travel agency to book the trip.

1010. Gebiet von touristischem Interesse = Area of tourist interest

Auf der rechten Seite sehen Sie ein Gebiet von touristischem Interesse.
On your right you will find an area of tourist interest.

1011. Informationsschalter = Information desk

Wir suchen den Informationsschalter.
We are looking for the information desk.

1012. Tourismusbüro = Tourism office

Das Tourismusbüro gibt immer die richtigen Informationen.

The tourism office always gives the right informations.

1013. Informationsbüro = Information office

Kannst du mir bitte zeigen, wo das Informationsbüro ist?
Can you show me where the information office is, please?

1014. Kasse = Ticket office

Die Kasse ist von 9:00 bis 17:00 Uhr geöffnet.
The ticket office is open from 9:00 a.m. to 5:00 p.m.

1015. Karte = Ticket

Der Preis für die Karte beträgt 150 Euro.
The ticket price is 150 euros.

1016. Bahnsteig 2 = Platform

Am Bahnsteig 2 einfahrender Zug, entfernen Sie sich von der gelben Linie.
Train arriving at platform 2, get away from the yellow line.

1017. Ziel = Destination

Mein Ziel ist Florenz.
My destination is Florence.

1018. Urlaub = Vacation

Paolo beginnt am Montag seinen Urlaub.
Paolo is starting his vacation on Monday.

1019. Halt = Stop

Mein Halt ist der nächste.
My stop is the next one.

1020. Reiseroute = Itinerary

Wir haben eine genaue Reiseroute zu befolgen.
We have an accurate itinerary to follow.

1021. Wagonnummer = Wagon number

Meine Wagonnummer ist 134
The number of my wagon is 134.

1022. Abteil = Compartment

Mein Abteil hat die Nummer 103.
My compartment is number 103.

1023. Haltestelle = Station

Der Bahnhof Mailand ist geschlossen.
The Milan station is closed.

1024. Bahnkarte = Railcard

Ich habe eine 2 Jahre gültige Bahnkarte.
I have a railcard valid for 2 years.

1025. Zug = Train

Der Zug, den Luca nahm, hatte Verspätung.
The train Luca took was late.

1026. Ausgehender Zug = Outbound train

Der ausgehende Zug fährt in 5 Minuten ab.
The outbound train leaves in 5 minutes.

1027. Rückzug = Return train

Der Rückzug fährt am 30. August um 12:50 Uhr ab.
The return train leaves on August 30th at 12:50 p.m.

1028. Wagen = Carriage

Der Wagen, in dem Paolo sitzt, ist der 15.
The carriage where Paolo is sitting is the 15th.

1029. Koffer = Suitcase

Der Koffer ist bereit, es ist Zeit zu gehen.
The suitcase is ready, it's time to leave.

1030. Geschwindigkeit = Speed

Die Geschwindigkeit der Züge von Frecciarossa ist sehr hoch.
The speed of the Frecciarossa trains is very high.

1031. Reise= Journey

Dies ist die schönste Reise meines Lebens.
This is the most beautiful journey of my life.

1032. Flugzeug = Plane

Das Flugzeug von Mailand nach London ist vor allem bei Geschäftsleuten sehr beliebt.

The Milan-London plane is a very popular line, especially among businessmen.

1033. Flughafen = Airport

Der Flughafen ist drei Kilometer von dem von uns gebuchten Hotel entfernt.
The airport is three kilometers away from the hotel we booked.

1034. Flugzeug = Aircraft

Das Flugzeug ist ein Boeing.
The aircraft is a boeing.

1035. Gepäckausgabe = Baggage claim area

Ich bin an der Gepäckausgabe.
I'm at the baggage claim area.

1036. Ankunftsbereich = Arrivals

Der Ankunftsbereich befindet sich im oberen Stockwerk.
The arrivals area is upstairs.

1037. Reiseversicherung = Travel insurance

Möchten Sie eine Reiseversicherung hinzufügen?
Do you want to add a travel insurance?

1038. Gepäck = Baggage

Das Gepäck darf nicht mehr als 20 Kilo wiegen, um einen Aufpreis zu vermeiden.

The baggage mustn't weigh more than 20 kilos to avoid paying a surcharge.

1039. Handgepäck = Hand luggage

Ich habe nur ein Handgepäck.
I only have a hand luggage.

1040. Aufgegebenes Gepäck = Checked baggage

Wir haben aufgegebenes Gepäck im Frachtraum.
We have luggage in the hold.

1041. Check-in-Schalter = Check-in desk

Der Check-in-Schalter befindet sich auf der rechten Seite.
The check-in desk is on the right.

1042. Gate = Gate

Das Gate Nummer 6 ist für den Flug 747 geöffnet.
Gate number 6 is open for flight 747.

1043. Annullierung = Cancellation

Sie informierten uns über die Annullierung der Flüge.
They informed us about the cancellation of the flights.

1044. Bordkarte = Boarding card

Bitte zeigen Sie mir Ihre Bordkarte.
Please show me your boarding card.

1045. Sicherheitsgurte = Seatbelt

Bitte legen Sie Ihre Sicherheitsgurte an.
Please fasten your seat belts.

1046. Sicherheit = Security

Es wurden zahlreiche Sicherheitskontrollen durchgeführt.
Numerous security checks have been carried out.

1047. Zoll = Customs

Der Zoll ist für Nicht-EEC-Bürger.
Customs is for non-EEC citizens.

1048. Zollfrei = Duty free

Dieses Produkt ist zollfrei.
This product is duty free.

1049. Freigepäckmenge = Baggage allowance

Wenn Ihr Gepäck mehr als 20 Kilo wiegt, müssen Sie eine Freigepäckmenge zahlen.
If your luggage exceeds 20 kilos, you must pay a baggage allowance.

1050. Abfluggate = Boarding gate

Ich suche nach dem Abfluggate.
I'm looking for the boarding gate.

1051. Boarding = Boarding

Das Boarding befindet sich unten links.

Boarding is at the bottom left.

1052. Fluggesellschaft = Airline

Welche Fluggesellschaft wirst du nehmen?
Which airline will you take?

1053. Förderband = Conveyor belt

Das Förderband ist kaputt.
The conveyor belt is broken.

1054. Flugnummer = Flight number

Sehen Sie sich bitte die Flugnummer genau an.
Look carefully at the flight number, please.

1055. Kurzzeitparkplatz = Short stay parking

Du musst dich über den Kurzzeitparkplatz erkundigen.
You need to inquire about the short stay parking.

1056. Langzeitparkplatz = Long stay parking

Da wir drei Wochen weg sind, müssen wir nach einem Langzeitparkplatz suchen.
Being away for three weeks, we have to look for long stay parking.

1057. Abflüge = Departures

Der Abflugbereich ist voll von Menschen, die in den Sommerurlaub reisen.

The departures area is full of people leaving for summer holidays.

1058. Landestreifen = Landing strip

Die Landestreifen sind besetzt, Sie können jetzt nicht landen.
The landing strip is busy, you can't land now.

1059. Verzögerung = Delay

Alle Flugzeuge, die über Europa fliegen, haben Verzögerungen erlitten.
All the planes flying above Europe have been delayed.

1060. Gepäckausgabe = Baggage claim

Wo ist die Gepäckausgabe?
Where is the baggage claim please?

1061. Zwischenstopp = Stopover

Ich werde einen Zwischenstopp in Amsterdam einlegen.
I will make a stopover in Amsterdam.

1062. Sitze auf der Gangseite = Seats on the corridor side

Das sind die Sitze auf der Gangseite.

1063. Fensterplatz = Window seat

Können Sie mir bitte einen Fensterplatz geben?
Can you give me a window seat, please?

1064. Büro für verlorenes Gepäck = Lost baggage office

Ich muss zum Büro für verlorenes Gepäck gehen, weil ich meinen orangefarbenen Koffer nicht mehr finden kann.
I must go to the lost baggage office because I can't find my orange suitcase anymore.

1065. Notausgänge = Emergency exits

Rechts und links von Ihnen befinden sich die Notausgänge.
On your right and left there are the emergency exits.

1066. Flug = Flight

Es gibt stündlich einen Flug.
There is a flight every hour.

1067. Fahrwerke = Landing gears

Sie befestigten die Fahrwerke an dem Flugzeug.
They attached the landing gears to the plane.

1068. Interkontinentalflüge = Intercontinental flight

Interkontinentalflüge dauern länger als acht Stunden.
Intercontinental flights are longer than eight hours.

1069. Inlandflug = National flight

Mit einem Inlandflug gelangt man von Mailand aus in einer Stunde nach Rom.

With a national flight you can get to Rome from Milan in one hour.

1070. Fahrkartenverkäufer = Ticket seller

Marco ist ein Fahrkartenverkäufer am Bahnhof.
Marco is a ticket seller at the station.

1071. Fahrkartenkontrolleur = Ticket inspector

Wo ist der Fahrkartenkontrolleur?
Where is the ticket inspector?

1072. Hotelmanager = Hotel manager

Der Hotelmanager geht immer sehr sorgfältig auf die Bedürfnisse seiner Kunden ein.
The hotel manager is always very careful to his costumers needs.

1073. Concierge = Concierge

Der Hotel-Concierge steht Ihnen für alle Informationen zur Verfügung.
The hotel concierge is at your disposal for any information.

1074. Nacht-Concierge = Night concierge

Wenn Sie spät zurückkommen, wird der Nacht-Concierge die Tür für Sie öffnen.
If you return late, there will be the night concierge to open the door.

1075. Reisebüro = Travel agent

Du musst zu meinem Reisebüro gehen.
You must go to my travel agent.

1076. Reiseleiter = Tour guide

Wir machen eine Führung mit einem Reiseleiter.
We have a tour with a tour guide.

1077. Rezeptionist = Receptionist

Der Rezeptionist muss Englisch können.
The receptionist must know English.

1078. Busfahrer = Bus driver

Der Busfahrer arbeitet im Schichtbetrieb.
The bus driver is a shift work.

1079. = Taxi driver

Luigi ist ein Taxifahrer in der Nacht.
Luigi is a night taxi driver.

1080. Flugbegleiter = Flight attendant

Luigi ist immer auf Reisen. Er ist ein Flugbegleiter.
Luigi always travels: he is a flight attendant.

1081. Gepäckträger = Porter

Brauchen Sie einen Gepäckträger für Ihr Gepäck, Ma'am?
Do you need a porter for your baggage, ma'am?

1082. Passagier = Passenger

Jeder Passagier bitte auf seinen Platz.
Each passenger reaches its place, please.

1083. Gepäckabfertiger = Baggage handler

Ich muss mit einem Gepäckabfertiger sprechen.
I need to talk to a baggage handler.

1084. Tourist = Tourist

Michele ist ein Tourist.
Michele is a tourist.

1085. Kapitän = Captain

Der Kapitän wünscht Ihnen eine angenehme Reise.
The captain wishes you a pleasant journey.

1086. Pilot = Pilot

Mario arbeitet als Pilot.
Mario works as a pilot.

1087. Audioguide = Audio-guide

Ich würde einen Audioguide zum besseren Verständnis der Ausstellung bevorzugen.
I would prefer an audio-guide to better understand the exhibition.

1088. Karte = Map

Die Karte ist nützlich, um sich besser orientieren zu können.

The map is useful to ensure a better bearing.

1089. Kunststädte = Art city

Kunststädte werden während der abendlichen Eröffnung der Museen von Touristen belagert.
Art cities are besiged by tourists during the musuems evening opening.

1090. Fußgänger = Pedestrian

Das Stadtzentrum ist eine Fußgängerzone.
The city centre is a pedestrian area.

1091. Führungen = Organized tours

Dieses Jahr organisierten sie viele Führungen, um dieses interessante Gebiet zu entdecken.
This year they organized many guided tours to discover this interesting area.

1092. Geschäftsreise = Business trip

Die Reise von Mario ist eine Geschäftsreise und kein Vergnügen, daher wird er nicht viel Zeit für einen Besuch der Stadt haben.
That of Mario is a business trip, not a pleasure one, so he won't have much time to visit the city.

1093. Bewertung = Review

Diese Hotelbewertungen sind nicht gut.
This hotel reviews are not good.

1094. Exkursionen = Excursions

Das Programm ist voller Exkursionen.
The program is rich of excursions.

1095. mieten = To rent

Wir müssen ein Auto mieten, um Apulien zu besuchen.
We need to rent a car to visit Apulia.

1096. Eine Reservierung stornieren = Cancel the reservation

Bitte, stornieren Sie meine Rreservierung im August.
Please, cancel my room reservation on August.

1097. abheben = To take off

Wir sind bereit, abzuheben, Kapitän.
We are ready to take off, captain.

1098. Landen = To land

Das Flugzeug landet auf der Notlandebahn.
The plane is landing on the emergency runway.

1099. aufbrechen = To leave

Morgen brechen wir nach Brasilien auf, und es wird eine aufregende dreiwöchige Reise sein.
Tomorrow we leave for Brazil and it will be an exciting three-week journey.

1100. Eine Reservierung bestätigen = Confirm the reservation

Ich rufe Sie an, um meine Reservierung für August zu bestätigen.
I'm calling you to confirm my reservation for August.

1101. Besuchen = To visit

Wir möchten diesen Sommer Schottland besuchen.
We would like to visit Scotland this summer.

BUSINESS
-
GESCHÄFTLICH

1102. Berufsausbildungszentrum = Professional training center

Ich muss in das Berufsausbildungszentrum gehen.
I have to go to the professional training center.

1103. Fabrik = Factory

Marco arbeitet in einer Fabrik.
Marco works in a factory.

1104. Aktivitäten = Activity

Beenden Sie alle Aktivitäten
Stop all the activities.

1105. Firma = Company

Für welche Firma arbeitet James?
What company does James work for?

1106. Filiale = Branch

Du musst in die Filiale gehen.
You must go to the branch.

1107. Holdinggesellschaft = Holding company

Dieses Unternehmen ist eigentlich eine Holdinggesellschaft.
That company is a holding company actually.

1108. Institut = Institution

Marco ging zum Inkassoinstitut.
Marco went to the debt collection institution.

1109. Kongresszentrum = Convention center

Kannst du mich zum Kongresszentrum bringen?
Can you take me to the convention center?

1110. Unternehmen = Company

Merlett ist ein sehr seriöses Unternehmen.
Merlett is a very serious company.

1111. Genossenschaft = Cooperative

Paolo arbeitet in einer Genossenschaft.
Paolo works in a cooperative.

1112. Auf Lager = Stock

Dieses Produkt ist nicht auf Lager.
That product is not in stock.

1113. Gesellschaft = Society

Es ist eine sterbende Gesellschaft.
It is a dying society.

1114. Steuerbehörde = Revenue agency

Die Steuerbehörde verklagte Michele.
The revenue agency sued Michele.

1115. Büro = Office

Morgens muss Marco im Büro sein.
In the morning Marco must be in the office.

1116. Hauptsitz = Headquarter

Der Hauptsitz von Amazon ist in Amerika.
Amazon's headquarters is in America.

1117. Ausbildung = Apprenticeship

Paolo macht eine Ausbildung.
Paolo is doing an apprenticeship.

1118. Vertrag = Contract

Hast du bereits einen Vertrag unterzeichnet?
Have you already signed a contract?

1119. Steuererklärung = Tax return

Hast du die Steuererklärung bereits ausgefüllt?
Have you already filled the tax return?

1120. Franchise = Franchise

Mark ist daran interessiert, dieses Franchise zu erwerben.
Mark is interested in acquiring that franchise.

1121. Regularien = Regulation

Es gibt Regularien, die eingehalten werden müssen.
There is a regulation that has to be respected.

1122. Kündigungsschreiben = Resignation letter

Jeff hat gestern sein Kündigungsschreiben abgegeben.
Jeff delivered his resignation letter yesterday.

1123. Gewinn- und Verlustrechnung = Income statement

Die Gewinn- und Verlustrechnung von Marco ist negativ.
Marco's income statement is negative.

1124. Veranstaltung = Stage

Diese Woche ist Lucas auf einer Veranstaltung.
This week Lucas is doing a stage.

1125. Rechnung = Bill

Haben sie dir die Rechnung gegeben?
Did they give you the bill?

1126. Lebenslauf = Resume

Der Lebenslauf ist wichtig, um Stellenangebote zu erhalten.
The resume is important to get job opportunities.

1127. Geschäftsplan = Business plan

Haben Sie den Geschäftsplan bereits gelesen?
Have you already read the business plan?

1128. System = System

Es ist ein komplexes System.
It is a complex system.

1129. Praktikanten = Trainee

Leute, ich stelle euch den neuen Praktikanten vor.
Guys, I present you the new trainee.

1130. Listenpreis = List

Der Listenpreis dieses Mobiltelefons beträgt 2900 Dollar.
The list price of that mobile phone is 2900 dollars.

1131. Lizenz = License

Haben Sie die Windows 10-Lizenz gekauft?
Have you purchased the Windows 10 license?

1132. Budget = Budget

Wie steht es mit dem Staatsbudget?
How's the state budget going?

1133. Vereinbarung = Agreement

Haben Sie die Vereinbarung unterzeichnet?
Have you signed the agreement?

1134. Organigramm = Organization chart

Wir werden ein Organigramm erstellen, um die Situation zu analysieren.
We will do an organization chart to analyze the situation.

1135. Geschäft = Deal

Schließen Sie dieses Geschäft sofort ab.

Conclude this deal immediately.

1136. Abonnement = Subscription

Worum geht es bei dem Abonnement?
What is the subscription about?

1137. Locher = Hole-puncher

Könnten Sie mir den Locher reichen?
Would you pass me the hole-puncher?

1138. gestanzte Mappen = Punched pocket folders

Wie viele gestanzte Mappen gibt es?
How many punched pocket folders are there?

1139. Ordner = Folder

Was ist in diesem Ordner?
What's in that folder?

1140. Kommode = Drawer

Der Hefter befindet sich in der Kommode.
The stapler is in the chest of drawers.

1141. Aufbewahrungskisten = Storage boxes

Legen Sie die Unterlagen in die Aufbewahrungskisten.
Put the documents in the storage boxes.

1142. Schreibtischorganisator = Desk organizer

Ein Schreibtischorganisator wäre notwendig.
A desk organizer would be necessary.

1143. Schreibtisch = Desk

Alles, was Sie brauchen, ist auf Ihrem Schreibtisch.
Everything you need is on your desk.

1144. Markierstift = Marker

Wo haben Sie den Markierstift hingelegt?
Where did you put the marker?

1145. Monitorständer = Monitor stand

Wo haben Sie den Monitorständer hingestellt?
Where did you put the monitor stand?

1146. Geschäftsmann = Businessman

Mario ist ein Geschäftsmann.
Mario is a businessman.

1147. Empfänger = Beneficiary

Wer wird der Empfänger der Überweisung sein?
Who will be the beneficiary of the transfer?

1148. Geschäftsfrau = Businesswoman

Die Zahl der Geschäftsfrauen wächst.
The businesswomen are growing in number.

1149. befristeter Arbeiter = Fixed-term worker

Mara ist eine befristete Arbeiterin.
Mara is a fixed-term worker.

1150. Büroangestellter = Office worker

Der Büroangestellte ist ein sesshafter Arbeiter.
The office worker is a sedentary work.

1151. Chef = Boss

Mein Chef ist heute nervös.
My boss is nervous today.

1152. Angestellter = Employee

Luca ist ein Staatsangestellter.
Luca is a state employee.

1153. Investor = Investor

Heute werden wir den Investor kennenlernen.
Today we will know the investor.

1154. Arbeiter = worker

Marco ist ein unermüdlicher Arbeiter.
Marco is a tireless worker.

1155. Freiberufler = Freelance

Andrea ist freiberuflich tätig.
Andrea is a freelancer.

1156. Gefeuert = Fired

Sie sind gefeuert!
You're fired!

1157. Fonds = Fund

Haben Sie Ihren Fonds zurückgezogen?
Have you withdrawn your fund?

1158. Analyse = Analysis

Es ist eine sehr interessante Analyse.
It's a very interesting analysis.

1159. Auktion = Auction

Sein Haus wird bei einer Auktion versteigert.
His house is at auction.

1160. Vorteil = Benefit

Ich überlasse Ihnen den Vorteil des Zweifels.
I leave you the benefit of the doubt.

1161. Newsletter = Newsletter

Haben Sie gehört, was im Newsletter steht?
Have you heard what the newsletter says?

1162. Budget = Budget

Welches Budget haben Sie?
What budget do you have?

1163. Wechselkurs = Exchange rate

Wie hoch ist der Euro-Dollar-Wechselkurs?
How much is the euro-dollar exchange rate?

1164. Produktionskapazität = Production capacity

Wie hoch ist die Produktionskapazität dieser Maschinen?
What is the production capacity of that machinery?

1165. Kapital = Capital

Welches gesellschaftliche Kapital hat Facebook? What social capital does Facebook have?

1166. Nettowert = Net worth

Der Nettowert dieses Unternehmens beträgt 3 Millionen Dollar.
The net worth of that company is 3 million dollars.

1167. Ethikkodex = Ethical code

Der Ethikkodex sollte in jedem von uns vorhanden sein.
The ethical code should be in each of us.

1168. Handel = Trade

Wie ist der Handel in Deutschland?
How is the trade in Germany?

1169. Genehmigung = Concession

Er hat die Genehmigung, den Laden zu eröffnen.
He's got the concession to open the shop.

1170. Verwaltungskontrollsoe = Management control

Wir werden eine Verwaltungskontrollsoftware herunterladen.
We will download a management control software.

1171. Schulden = Debt

Wie hoch sind die Staatsschulden?
How much is the public debt?

1172. Kaution = Deposit

Ich habe das Geld auf der Kaution hinterlegt.
I left the money at the deposit.

1173. Nachfrage = Demand

In diesem Sektor deckt sich die Nachfrage mit dem Angebot.
In this sector the demand coincides with the offer.

1174. Wirtschaftswissenschaften = Economics

Studierst du noch Wirtschaftswissenschaften?
Are you still studying economics?

1175. Steuern = Tax

Trevor hat Steuern hinterzogen.
Trevor has evaded tax.

1176. Arbeitskraft = Workforce

Diese Männer bieten dem Unternehmen eine riesige Arbeitskraft.
Those men offer the company a huge workforce.

1177. Spaltung = Split

Das Unternehmen hat eine Spaltung vorgenommen.
The company made a split.

1178. Fusionieren = Merge

Hast du gehört, dass WhatsApp mit Instagram fusioniert ist?
Have you heard that WhatsApp merged with Instagram?

1179. Garantie = Warranty

Ich habe eine 3-Jahres-Garantie auf diesen Fernseher.
I have a 3-year warranty on this television.

1180. Verwaltung = Management

Haben Sie die Verwaltungssoftware heruntergeladen?
Have you downloaded the management software?

1181. Gruppe = Group

Eine Gruppe von Investoren ist gestern eingetroffen.
A group of investors arrived yesterday.

1182. Verdienst = Earning

Wie hoch ist dein monatlicher Verdienst?
What is your monthly earning?

1183. Grundstück = Property

Wie viel haben Sie für dieses Grundstück bezahlt?
How much did you pay for that property?

1184. Belastung = Imposition

Wie hoch ist die Belastung?
How much is the imposition?

1185. Steuer = Tax

Es wurde eine Steuer von 22% erhoben.
A 22% tax was applied.

1186. Einkommenssteuer = Income tax

Es wird eine Einkommenssteuer erhoben.
An income tax will be applied.

1187. = Task

Welche Aufgabe wurde Ihnen zugewiesen?
What task was assigned to you?

1188. Index = Index

Hast du den Sparindex gelesen?
Have you read the savings index?

1189. Innovationen = Innovation

In den letzten Jahren hat es viele Innovationen gegeben.
In recent years there have been many innovations.

1190. Zinssatz = Interest rate

Wie hoch ist der Zinssatz?
What is the interest rate?

1191. Investition = Investment

Wie ist diese Investition gelaufen?
How did that investment go?

1192. Markteinführung = Launch

Der Preis bei der Markteinführung dieses Tablets beträgt 1099 Dollar.
The price at the launch of that tablet is 1099 dollars.

1193. Beruf = Job

Welchen Beruf übt Marco aus?
What job does Marco do?

1194. Leasing = Leasing

Marco hat ein Auto per Leasing gekauft.
Marco bought a car with leasing.

1195. Limit = Limit

Wie hoch ist das tägliche Einzugslimit?
How much is the daily collection limit?

1196. Ladung = Batch

Wir haben eine Ladung Obst gekauft.

We bought a batch of fruit.

1197. Maschine = Machinery

Die Maschine ging kaputt.
The machinery broke.

1198. Marge = Margin

Die Gewinnmarge ist sehr hoch.
The profit margin is very high.

1199. Rohmaterial = Raw material

Das Rohmaterial ist fast fertig.
The raw material is almost finished.

1200. Hypothek = Mortgage

Wir müssen eine Hypothek aufnehmen, um das Haus zu kaufen.
We need to get a mortgage to buy that house.

1201. Nische = Niche

Es ist ein Nischensektor.
It is a niche sector.

1202. Verpflichtung = Obligation

Der Vertrag enthält eine Verpflichtung.
There is an obligation in the contract.

1203. Angebot = Offer

In diesem Sektor deckt sich die Nachfrage mit dem Angebot.
In this sector, the demand coincides with the offer.

1204. Maßnahme = Operation

Welche Maßnahme haben Sie gestern durchgeführt?
What operation did you do yesterday?

1205. Zahlung = Payment

Die Zahlung war erfolgreich.
The payment was successful.

1206. Beteiligung = Participation

Haben Sie von seiner Beteiligung gehört?
Have you heard about his participation?

1207. Verlust = Loss

Diesen Monat haben wir einen Verlust gemacht.
This month we are in loss.

1208. = Presentation

Paolo hält einen Vortrag.
Paolo is giving a presentation.

1209. = Loan

Ich habe gestern um ein Darlehen gebeten.
I asked for a loan yesterday.

1210. = Productivity

Produktivität ist die Grundlage eines erfolgreichen Unternehmens.
Productivity is the foundation of a successful company.

1211. Anteil = Share

Ich habe einen Anteil an dieser Firma.
I have a share of that company.

1212. Preisangebot = Quote

Ich habe gerade ein Preisangebot gemacht.
I just made a quote.

1213. Verhältnis = Ratio

Das Preis-Leistungs-Verhältnis ist ausgezeichnet.
The quality/price ratio is excellent.

1214. Einkommen = Income

Marco erhält die das Bürgerschaftseinkommen.
Marco receives the citizenship income.

1215. Leistung = Performance

Die Leistung dieses Monats ist ausgezeichnet.
This month's performance is excellent.

1216. Rückstufung = Demotion

Jede Rückstufung wird ein Fehlschlag sein.
Any demotion will be a failure.

1217. Steigend = Upward

Der Kurs dieser Aktie ist steigend.
The price of that stock is upward.

1218. Einnahmen = Earning

Was sind die heutigen Einnahmen?
What is today earning?

1219. Risiko = Risk

Es ist eine Operation mit hohem Risiko.
It's a high-risk operation.

1220. Ersparnisse = Saving

Er hat seine gesamten Ersparnisse für den Kauf eines Bootes verwendet.
He used all his savings to buy a boat.

1221. Besprechung = Meeting

Stören Sie Lucia nicht, sie ist in einer Besprechung.
Do not disturb Lucia, she is in a meeting.

1222. Gehalt = Salary

Welches Gehalt bekommt Luke monatlich?
What salary does Luke receive monthly?

SOME FINAL ADVICE FROM JOHN

We've reached the end of this book. And I have good news and bad news for you. The good news is that your vocabulary has been greatly enriched and you will surely be able to hold a conversation in German without any major difficulties!

You are now ready to face new experiences, for example you can take that trip around the world that you have always postponed or apply for that job abroad without fear of not knowing the language.

Now let's move on to the bad news. Your journey doesn't end here. If you thought this book was all you would need to become a native speaker, I'm very sorry.

As a matter of fact, you really never stop learning a language. Surely this book is a great start to your journey, but you can certainly improve further.

We studied different words during the course of this book, surely now you won't have any more problems when making a restaurant reservation, having a job interview or engaging in a simple conversation with a tourist you just met!

I would like to give you some pieces of advice that will be of great help in continuing this journey of studying the English language.

I highly recommend the following activities:

- **WATCH ENGLISH MOVIES**

You can begin with English subtitles if you have difficulties, progressing to watching with German subtitles, and finally sticking to watching movies in Geman without subtitles.

If after finishing a movie you feel like you didn't understand anything, don't get demoralized and above all don't give up. Watch the same movie several times until you understand it.

I know it sounds boring, but I guarantee you'll get great results soon.

- **DON'T ABANDON THIS BOOK ON A SHELF**

Go through this book again and again, take notes, study it, in short, remember that this book is not a novel. It is a handbook and as such I advise you to constantly have it within reach and go over it multiple times.

- **DOWNLOAD APPLICATIONS LIKE BABBEL OR DUOLINGO**

We live in the digital age with more opportunities than 30 years ago!

We must take advantage of the various resources at our disposal, among which I would recommend "Babbel" and "Duolingo": two applications that you can download on your smartphone and use to practice and improve your German language skills.

- **LISTEN TO GERMAN AUDIOBOOKS**

Did you know that Audible has a 30-day free trial? I wouldn't pass up that chance if I were you! Audiobooks are perfect, especially if you're a busy person. You can improve your listening and pronunciation while at the gym or in the car!

Finally, thank you very much for buying my book and I hope you enjoyed it.

Printed in Great Britain
by Amazon